TRAGIC HERO

PICKING UP THE PIECES

Published by Impact Publishing®, Lake Mary, FL.

Impact Publishing® is a registered trademark.

Printed in the United States of America.

Text by Autumn Jade Monroe

ISBN: 978-1-7369881-9-0
LCCN: 2022907620

This publication is designed to provide accurate and authoritative information with regard to the subject matter covered. It is sold with the understanding that the publisher is not engaged in rendering legal, accounting, or other professional advice. If legal advice or other expert assistance is required, the services of a competent professional should be sought. The opinions expressed by the authors in this book are not endorsed by Impact Publishing® and are the sole responsibility of the author rendering the opinion.

Most Impact Publishing® titles are available at special quantity discounts for bulk purchases for sales promotions, premiums, fundraising, and educational use. Special versions or book excerpts can also be created to fit specific needs.

For more information, please write:
Impact Publishing®
P.O. Box 950370
Lake Mary, FL 32795
Tel: 1.877.261.4930

TRAGIC HERO

PICKING UP THE PIECES

By

WALLY BRESSLER
with **Autumn Jade Monroe**

Impact Publishing®
Lake Mary, Florida

For my children:
MaryFrances, Emma, Alex, and Caroline,
there is no end to my love for all of you.

Always remember–anything is possible;
you can do anything!

"Wally takes an honest look within and embarks on a journey of his heartache, failure, and bounce off of rock bottom that has ultimately led him to success. His candor calls us to face the reality of our lives and take radical responsibility for where we are and where we want to go. A champion of his own story, Wally seeks to inspire others, no matter where they happen to be, to remember from within lies the power to rewrite the past through the successes of the present."

Nick Nanton
Co-Founder, CEO DNA Films
22-Time Emmy Award-Winning Director and Host

"During my 5+ years of hosting Mr. Biz Radio, I have interviewed 100s of fantastic people with amazing stories, but Wally's story is an absolute must-read if you want to be a better version of your current self. From a difficult childhood to a federal penitentiary, to trying to end his own life, to ... massive success! He refused to be a victim; instead, he chose to be a hero! Moreover, Wally does not *fake the funk* in this book; he draws on his own personal, real-life experiences to provide a blueprint you can use to positively impact all aspects of *your* life!"

"Mr. Biz" a.k.a. Ken Wentworth
Founder, Mr. Biz Solutions

"Too many so-called *sales experts* have written books that retell the same old, tired sales techniques. Not Wally Bressler! Wally's new book, *Tragic Hero*, will grab you by the throat; it will make you wonder how *Young Wally* ever managed to become *Wally the Mentor and Coach*. He not only made that transformation, he tells his story, brings you along for the journey, and explains how he helps businesspeople and salespeople succeed today."

Dave Kurlan
CEO, Objective Management Group

"As a person that has lived over half my life in a victim mentality, I resonated with *Tragic Hero* right away. If we have lived it, been imprisoned by it, survived through it and thrived after it, then we must share our stories to empower others going through it now. Wally does just that in his book and I applaud him for his extreme bravery; stepping up to the plate and sharing his incredibly vulnerable intimate experiences in order to empower other people. If you are ready to rewrite your past through the successes of your present, then I strongly urge you to pick up this book and start reading it immediately!"

Jason Tracey
Founder, Roar Consulting, Inc.

"Wally Bressler has been a friend of mine for over 20 years. He's a sales champion with a gift for teaching and a master at personal transformation. He will help you smash your limiting beliefs! Buy this book and thrive!"

Brent Gove, Realtor®
Real Estate Expert
Brent Gove and Associates powered by eXp
#2 Revenue Share Earner with eXp Realty

"I've worked alongside Wally Bressler for the better part of the last decade, and I've seen how impactful his approach to coaching people can be. His superpower is knowing the right questions to ask people in order to help them achieve incredible breakthroughs in their lives and businesses. This book details everything he's conquered to become the servant-minded coach and leader he is today. If you're looking for a blueprint on how to create time freedom, money freedom, and location freedom in your life–and are willing to take *radical responsibility* for what's going on in the six inches between your ears–you'll get it from Wally in this book."

Clifford Freeman, Jr., Realtor®
Real Estate Expert
President/CEO, The Cliff Freeman Group, brokered by eXp
#5 Revenue Share Earner with eXp Realty

"I've known Wally since 2006 when we were on NBC's The Biggest Loser together. I have always admired Wally's ability to inspire, motivate, and empower people. This book is the next evolution of that empowerment. His transparency will give you, and others, the courage to use adversity to their advantage. A must-read!"

Ken Canion
CEO, Brand Specialist
The Ken Canion Group

"Full disclosure ... Wally Bressler is my friend. We have a long history together dating back to late summer 1986 when we both showed up as freshmen football players at Hamilton College in Central New York. I've seen Wally at his very best, and I've remained steadfast through the toughest times of his life. His journey of self-discovery has taken him down paths–many of his own choosing–that would have broken a lesser spirit. And through this adversity, the walls that were built as self-protection over years of trials and challenges were torn down as Wally's courageous vulnerability allowed him to rebuild his life. Yes, Wally Bressler is my friend, but he is also an inspiration in my life. And through this book, I believe he can be in your life as well."

Herb Hand
Offensive Line Coach
University of Central Florida

"I've seen Wally Bressler at his absolute best and worst over the last 16 years. Despite everything that's happened to him and what he's put himself through, he's never given up. His talent as a coach and trainer is unparalleled because of the wisdom he's gained through facing and overcoming the challenging times he's dealt with in his life. His book will inspire you to face any obstacle with the confidence you need to never give up no matter how tough things get. If you're plagued with self-sabotage, low self-esteem, low self-worth, perfectionism, or even a business that is just not growing, *Tragic Hero* is a must-read."

Jay Kinder, Realtor®
Real Estate Expert
Co-founder, National Association of Expert Advisors
#7 Revenue Share Earner with eXp Realty

"I recommend that everyone get this book and embrace what Wally has to say and teach! Wally has opened his heart and soul to expose his demons and how he has overcome tremendous obstacles to find himself, and become the best version of himself. He's also helped countless others overcome their deep-rooted fears–fears that hold them back from moving forward and grabbing life by the neck and saying to it: *I will not be denied living life as a positive, super successful person.* I know this because at 70 years old, Wally helped me recapture my MOJO and my desire and drive to be the best after years of self-doubt. Let Wally help you find your true self. He will help you identify what's holding you back and then get ready to soar! Get on the Wally train and let him help you get to your ultimate destination."

Jim McClain, Sr., Realtor®
Real Estate Expert
President, McClain Realty Group brokered by eXp

"As a digital marketing expert, I run into people daily who are unable to pick up the phone to grow their business, which is unfortunate because even today, we still need to use the phone to make sales. A short while ago, I hired Wally to coach a group of 10 digital marketers from my inner circle on how to overcome self-sabotage, perfectionism, procrastination, and call reluctance. In this book, you'll learn what he shared with them to help change their businesses and lives forever. There is no challenge TOO big to overcome and Wally will inspire you to see any problem as an opportunity by the time you're finished reading the book. Pick this book up and don't put it down until you're done! Then flip it over and read it again!"

Jeff Lopez
CEO, PLUSPLUS® MEDIA INC.

"Wally was my first growth coach in the real estate business. He, by far, had the largest impact on my sales growth and mindset of anyone I have worked with within the real estate industry. He gave me confidence in making business decisions that I wouldn't have made otherwise. Wally single-handedly took me from $5 million in sales volume to $35 Million in sales volume in less than 3 years. In this book, you'll see that Wally not only helps in business growth, he also has a heart of gold and truly cares for others. He wants the best for everyone and enjoys having a positive impact and making a difference in people's lives."

Kyle Davis, Realtor ®
Real Estate Expert
President, Kyle Davis Real Estate Experts
Keller Williams Mullinix
#2 Team in Oklahoma for Sales Volume
#8 Team in Oklahoma for Total Sides Sold

"Wally Bressler is the ultimate performance coach and mentor. Under his leadership, we were able to triple our revenue in less than three years. Results like this don't come from learning more tactics or techniques. They come from clearing out the psychological barriers that are holding you back from achieving your greatest potential. Wally has the innate ability to not only understand what is creating your limitations, but also recognize with love and compassion how to dissolve them and create a brighter path forward. Wally's vulnerability, transparency, and dedication to others allow those around him to be impacted in the most positive and unbelievable ways. This book will help those who are hiding from their own darkness to bring out their light so they may shine like never before."

Kristy Moore, Realtor®
Real Estate Expert
Broker-Owner
Local Expert Realty

"I've had the honor to know and work with Wally for almost 2 decades now. Wally is one of the most knowledgeable, straightforward, and most caring human beings I know. As you'll learn in this book, it's Wally's wealth of knowledge and experience in not only coaching people in business and life but also in coaching himself through any situation that's put him in a position where he has not seen a constraint personally or professionally that he hasn't been able to work through. I first worked with Wally in a professional setting when he coached our real estate team to become better agents and better humans making our team one of the best in the marketplace through his guidance and coaching. When I personally started coaching, Wally was one of the key reasons I was able to easily develop the skills needed to become a world-class coach myself. Whatever Wally is teaching, whatever he is sharing, whatever he's coaching, it is absolutely worth your time and attention because I promise he's going to help you become a better human which in return will make your business better."

John Kitchens, Realtor®
Real Estate Expert
Chief Legacy Officer
Coach Code®

"I started working with Wally in the winter of 2021 and I had no idea at that point how much my life was going to change for the better. I joined his Phone Sales Secrets program and although it was challenging in terms of facing my inner demons, it's something I had to do as they were holding me back both personally and professionally. Using lessons and strategies covered in this book, we tapped into my deep-rooted fear of rejection and failure. I remember about halfway through it was like a switch flipped and things started changing for me. I wasn't afraid to pick up the phone anymore and rejection wasn't so scary. The biggest change was I was no longer afraid of being successful. I learned so much about business and how to be better and do better, but I made some incredible personal gains as well thanks to what Wally shares here in *Tragic Hero*. Thank you Wally for always being an open book, for understanding the complexities within a person, and for being an amazing coach. I will truly never forget what you taught me."

Ashley Hutchison, Realtor [®]
Real Estate Expert
Concept Realty Group, Inc.

"Like Wally, I had hit absolute rock bottom. I had learned bad habits from childhood. I had a burning hatred for myself that caused me to make poor decisions. I led myself to believe that my best would never be good enough and the good things in life would always be just out of reach. Before I met Wally, depression saturated every aspect of my life. My life was controlled by a rage and tear-filled version of me no one had seen before. I was fixated on how I presented to the world; perfection was everything. Having one hair out of place resulted in a spiral of self-doubt and self-loathing. I could never look beyond what I knew in life because I was too scared to take a risk for greatness. With Wally's help and direction (that was based on the same amazing information you'll find in this book) I was able to take control of my life and start to uncover my real self. That real self is kind, fiercely independent, and successful. The lessons Wally shares in *Tragic Hero* taught me where to find my fire and how to utilize it to catapult me into wild success. Through Wally's teachings, I learned to unwind my negative thought pattern and discover how to heal from the traumatic events in my life. I am forever grateful for Wally's guidance and the many lessons he's taught me along the way."

Shelby Sieppert, Realtor®
Real Estate Expert
Concept Realty Group, Inc.

"As a fearless child, I seriously believed I could do anything. I was invincible. Then tragedy struck with an abusive father, crippling cancer deaths in my family, and a devastating divorce. I found myself vulnerable and hiding from the pain. That trauma led to me hiding from the phone. Unable to regain the success I once had in Real Estate, I enrolled in Wally's Sales Call Reluctance class. Instead of the usual tactics I hear taught, Wally brought me to a realization of what was actually happening. He helped me recognize the source of my fear … bad news comes through the phone! Wally taught me techniques to retrain my mind and changes occurred. My sales career is the best it's been in years. Dive into this book and unlock your hidden potential!

Danielle Lang, Realtor®
Real Estate Expert
Original Realty Co.

CONTENTS

ACKNOWLEDGMENTS

I've never believed that there is such a thing as a self-made man. I was only able to get through everything I've experienced in life because of the people who loved me even when I didn't love myself. I'd like to thank God for helping me get through all of the pain and suffering I caused to myself and others. Even during my darkest days, He was there to love me, support me and give me hope.

To my aunt and uncle, Pat and Roger Martin, *thank you*. You've been like second parents to me since I was a young boy–I love you both.

Stacie Bressler, thank you for being such an amazing mother to our children, a great co-parent, a good friend, and most importantly, for forgiving me for hurting you as deeply as I did.

Paul and David, you two have been my best friends in Texas since we met in 2010. I don't know if I would have made it through the time before, during, and after I went to prison without you. You are two amazing, Godly men and I'm grateful to have you in my life.

Chris, you are my longest-standing friend – my brother as much as my best friend. We've been through everything together; I know I'm a better person because of you.

Kelly, you literally saved my life. I've worked with scores of therapists and personal coaches, but you were the one who was able to meet me where I needed to be met and guide me through the worst time of my life. You are an angel sent from God and I will be forever grateful to you.

Steve Frank, Paul Adey, and Mike Davis, the three of you had a huge impact on me as a young man and helped shape me in more positive ways than I can articulate. I consider myself blessed to have been coached by the three of you while I was at Hamilton College and to still have you in my life 36 years later.

Bob Demello, you've been gone from this world for 20 years, but you were one of the first people who believed in me and helped me believe in myself. Know that you are missed by your family and friends; and that your kindness, generosity and live through me and countless others.

Herb Hand, you've been such an amazing friend and brother for the last 36 years. You've seen me at my worst and you've always been there for me when I've needed you. Thank you for being the great man and person that you are.

Bob Benish, even in my mid 20s, I was lost and out of place in corporate America. You were one of the few people to take the time to mentor and show an interest in me. I'm grateful for what I learned about writing, marketing and life from you.

Lisa Richardson, you helped me out emotionally, financially, and even with a car to drive so I could get around and not need to borrow one from someone else any longer. You truly live life with a servant's heart and I appreciate you.

I'd also like to thank all of the people who supported my family and me while I was away in prison: Susan Lord, Jim Keaty, Kristy Moore, Will Chow, Aaron Sather, Jon Perrera, Shawn Lane, Troy Baker, Mark Turman, Bill Witlash, Jeff Cook, Albie Stasek, Hassan Williams, Jill Hoover, Eddie Urso, Nick Kellar, Don Walters, Mick McAllister, Scott Cameron, Greg Wilson, Eric and Shelby Grey, and Michael and Eileen Hicks.

From a business perspective, I would not be able to do what I do today without the help, support, guidance, patience, and input of so many people throughout the years.

Jay Kinder and Michael Reese, not only did you give me a job when I needed it the most, but you supported my family while I was away in prison. You also helped me return to work when I came home from prison–without judgment. I will be forever grateful to both of you.

Amber Kinder, thank you for working with Jay and me to let me come home from prison and stay at your house. I had nowhere to go at that time and you and Jay made all the difference in how I restarted my life when I got back to Texas in 2014. There is no end to my gratitude for how you supported me.

Brian Moses, you gave me my first job in the real estate business and taught me so many things that have helped me succeed, and allowed me to help others succeed, over the last 24 years. I'm forever grateful for the opportunities that working with and learning from you afforded me.

Jeff Lopez, you gave me the support, confidence, and direction I needed to lay a strong foundation for Phone Sale Secrets–a business that now helps people change their lives every day. You said that I probably would have figured it out by myself, but I know things wouldn't have turned out as amazingly well without your direction and support.

Clifford Freeman, you and your family, Karen, Clifford III, and Caroline have made me feel like I'm part of your family as we've worked to build The Cliff Freeman Group. Thanks for all you've done for me and for being so generous with your time, love, and resources. You live life with a servant's heart and I'm blessed to call you my friend.

Doug Turner, you've been such a kind, loving man. You've done so much for me to make sure that I knew that I was loved, and to put me in a position to take care of my family. You are one of the most amazing people I know.

Scott and Shera Cameron, thank you for helping me get a place to live and transportation for myself after I came home from prison. You made my transition home immeasurably easier.

Mark Howard, Brittany Elliot and Jeff Daniel Clark, you all helped me through some of the toughest times in my life. Your guidance and patience were invaluable to me as I worked through them. Thank you for everything.

Thanks also to Kyle and Charlie Davis, Brian O'Neill, Don Zappia, Brett Jennings, Melisa Hatfield, Paul Glasgow, Mike Oddo, Jake Houle, Mark and Megan McManus, John Kitchens, Hollie Kitchens, Rachel Cahill, Kristy Moore, Kathleen Forrest, Jonathan Hoff, Jeff Quiane, Miranda Hayden, Shannon and Kimberly Lillard, for being there to support me through the tough times since I returned home from prison.

To all of the amazing people who took the time to write an endorsement for my book, I am eternally grateful for your time and thoughtfulness.

Nick Nanton and Angie Swenson, thank you and your team from Celebrity Press for helping make my dream of becoming a published author possible. Your experience, support, and input have been an invaluable part of this process.

Special thanks to the folks at Story Terrace, especially my editor, Elizabeth DiPietro for her incredible input and direction and Marleigh Green for getting me in touch with Autumn Jade Monroe.

I'm writing this acknowledgment last, not because it's the least important, but because I want it to stand out on its own:

Autumn Jade Monroe, I would have never been able to write this book without you. Your intuition, poetic mind, and writing style were the perfect match for me to tell my story. You and I are going to inspire people and help change their lives for years to come through this book. Thank you so very much for helping make this book a reality.

INTRODUCTION

I am not a victim.

Before you read this book, it's important for you to understand this. If you are familiar with my coursework or have done coaching with me—you know this is my mantra. I reiterate it verbally in every possible way throughout my curriculum ... *never often enough, in my opinion!* I emphasize this because as much as my story is one of redemption and what I did to overcome a lifetime of difficult and painful experiences, it's also about the things I did, to myself and others, that put me on a one-way trip to rock bottom.

I didn't realize, in my younger years, that thoughts and behaviors do not exist in a vacuum. Negative beliefs yield poor choices and poor choices yield ugly consequences. Though I made it through my 20s and 30s evading penalties by the skin of my teeth. I was eventually held accountable for the things I did ... and even more so, for the things I *neglected* to do. When it comes to personal development, there is no *cutting corners*—every part of ourselves must be accounted for. Nothing comes out in the wash. While we might find generous moments of recourse and the opportunity to make amends, we must all, at some point, take radical responsibility for our lives. Moreover, we must value our lives and *ourselves* enough to realize something— this personal onus is not a burden. It is an invaluable gift.

I wasn't in full understanding of that gift on September 5th, 2013, when I was stripped of my clothes and given a white jumpsuit that I couldn't zip up to cover my 475-pound frame, as I was logged in as inmate 12331-049 of FCI Forrest City. You would have thought that standing there, with a blank expression, having my mugshot taken for fraud would have been my *rock bottom* ... but I was stubborn.

Despite my 366-night stay, I still had so much further to fall. The mental prison of my vices that had shackled me since childhood eventually landed me in a federal penitentiary. My vices began as all insidious things do—in the private cell of my own mind, in a space of isolation that was seemingly innocuous—my childhood bedroom.

At six years old, my parents' demons were already catching up with me and it wouldn't be long before my addictions to food, money, sex, pornography and *lying* were cemented—all before my teenage years.

My vices first manifested in little ways—sneaking food, zoning out to television and video games and telling white lies that kept me out of trouble for larger issues—binge eating, the compulsive use of pornography and acting out violently in school.

Though my dad was a disciplinarian, I had low impulse control—and his abrasive parenting tactics only made me afraid of him for so long. Then ... I became defiant. By grammar school, I was spinning out internally. Externally, I was always in the guidance counselor's office. No one could figure out why 12-year-old Walter Bressler could not behave. Not even I could fully comprehend it.

It would take several decades for me to understand the ramifications of holding a reservoir of family secrets. Through countless failures and periods of reprieve, I would learn that trauma stores itself in the body and the small habits that marked me as a child would maim my life, sanity and personal relationships as an adult. Until finally, on a cool fall night in October of 2019 ... I decided I was going to take my own life.

Clearly—I didn't succeed. But I was breaths away when a pivotal turn of events gave me the last-minute, insatiable desire to *fight* for my life.

It was at that moment that I recognized my life was full of things that were outside of my control, but the one thing I had control over was my mind and willpower. Sure, things that had happened to me as a very young child were downright horrible. Even now, as a 53-year-old man, I'm remembering things that have been tucked away in my subconscious since I was very young. But there was a recognizable shift— around the age of 13—that I cannot ignore. At some point, my life became more about self-inflicted wounds than the physical, mental and emotional beatings I'd taken from the people in my life.

In fact, I would spend the majority of my life reliving old patterns and projecting my past trauma onto present situations, until the need for healing was so strong that I began to pay attention. Plagued by low self-esteem, low self-worth and extreme self-loathing, it took me roughly 45 years to sincerely seek counseling as a way to heal my extreme internal pain. There, I began to learn about the sources of my personal pain and the generational pain that preceded me. My parents were not perfect, but they tried their best with the tools they were given—they chain-smoked through the hard parts of their lives, demonstrated poor eating habits and handled their money poorly. Their parents had been fear-driven people who took their frustrations out on their kids and their kids took it out on my siblings and me. In retrospect, it was a miracle that I didn't choose to take my life and even more astounding was what I built thereafter.

If there's one thing I can say about myself, it's that I've always been *the black sheep*. It used to scare my pedantic mother to death. *What's Wally gone and gotten himself into now?* My parents were adamant about me using my college degree to better myself through a traditional nine-to-five job. They wanted me to have the guarantee of a consistent paycheck, with the promise of benefits and a 401k. But I was naturally enthusiastic and I was sick of slogging hours at someone else's sales desk. I'd had my fill of *keeping my hair short for the man* and wearing button-ups for a compensation package that was great but paled in comparison to what I would earn as an entrepreneur. Despite my short stint with fraudulent activity ... I knew I had a business mind. I also knew all the ways not to handle money—*and what to never do again.*

More than anything, I wanted the lessons I'd learned to be of service to other people. After working through my people-pleaser tendencies in therapy, I learned I wanted *to help* people and I could finally do so in a way that didn't compromise my mental wellbeing. So, with help and guidance from digital marketing expert, Jeff Lopez, I launched Phone Sales Secrets in 2021 and I am now helping people like me to work through their mental blocks and succeed in business and in life.

The secret I share with my clients, you ask? Well, it begins by dismantling the victim mentality.

Say it with me—

I am not a victim.

Yes, we all may have been a victim at one time in our lives. And to that point, it's likely not our fault how we got into the sad, painful place where we currently live. However, once we realize that we are in a bad place as a result of what happened to us, it becomes our responsibility to make the changes we need to live happy, fulfilling lives. As part of what I do, I walk clients through a program that helps them examine the internal shame that is keeping them from being able to pick up the phone and connect with potentially life-changing business opportunities.

What I've learned throughout the years is that shame is the silent killer of our ability to thrive in the workplace. It affects everything from monetary negotiations to time management as well as scaling and preserving integral business relationships. The thought process we maintain at home reveals itself in how we engage with our work. Do we pursue purpose-driven, fulfilling work that we love and that pays us well—because we *are certain* we deserve it? If the answer is *no*, it is most likely rooted in some sort of psychological block and most certainly—shame.

In my courses, we get vulnerable—and trust me, I recognize that can be scary. I am someone who has been to federal prison, who can still acknowledge that being truly seen by another person is terrifying. But I also did everything in my power to get around being vulnerable in the world and it resulted in consecutive, abysmal failures. So, I teach my clients how to present themselves with authentic confidence while facing rejection. When it happens—and it does for all brave risk-takers—I encourage my clients to keep wiggling the handles of opportunity until they find *their doors.* Together, we press on to new possibilities. We grieve. We celebrate. We mature. We heal. By nursing the grievous wounds that once victimized us, we are able to strengthen our minds to fuel our victories.

We are a band of victorious, *tragic heroes*—rewriting our pasts through the successes of our present. We recognize that while we are still on this earth, we are the main characters of our own stories—so we take radical responsibility to write the endings ... through all of the pain, with astounding mental fortitude and above all things—perseverance.

1

RADICAL RESPONSIBILITY

Eliminating the Victim Mentality

L ike all things deep-seated and subconscious, the victim mentality is cultivated through nature and nurture. In my case, it was generational. My parents learned it from their parents and it's the only thing I knew growing up.

One of the most unfortunate parts of adulthood is becoming disenchanted with even the best attributes of our parents. We grow up and realize; *they are imperfect* and we are forced to contend with their humanity. With complete compassion, I say—*my mom and dad had a limited skill set.* All parents do ... and while some parents do their best to figure it out, others devolve and give way to their vices. Mine fell into the latter camp.

My dad's most challenging addiction was *control.* For that matter, so was my mom's. They took turns with what they controlled, but usually when something didn't go exactly as they wanted—they'd yell. A lot. My dad and mom were hypercritical of many people and things in their lives ... especially their children and themselves. Sometimes, things seemed to devolve into bullying: *Do it because I said so*, which was usually followed by getting yelled at or a smack. The backhand to the face with the ring hand was especially unnerving. The fact that my parents were harder on themselves than on anyone else took me a long time to realize. It wasn't until adulthood that I learned that most people who have control issues and who are bullies don't have great self-esteem. My dad certainly didn't. And my mom's neuroticism didn't help.

The push and pull of their marriage became a dynamic dance of both of them trying to manage *everything* around them at all times. My mom was a real Chicken Little. The sky was *always* falling. There was no such thing as a *best-case* scenario. There was only the *worst possible outcome* ... and the slight chance we'd survive unscathed. As a result, Little Wally grew up with a lot of anxiety and bottled emotions. Born to two people who were constantly attempting to manage their internal states by controlling their external circumstances—my brain recorded those patterns as survival and I carried them into my adult years. And unfortunately ... they wouldn't be the only things I took with me.

Popular research in epigenetics teaches us that we carry generational trauma in our bodies. If our families struggled with systematic oppression, poverty, addiction, abuse, or neglect—the DNA of subsequent generations adapts as a response. The chemical reaction that takes place in our body changes our physiology, meaning two generations later—grandchildren can still be *adapting* to the traumas of their grandparents. Mark Wolynn addresses this idea in *It Didn't Start with You: How Inherited Family Trauma Shapes Who We Are and How to End the Cycle.* He writes,

"We learn about epigenetic changes—the chemical modifications that occur in our cells as a result of a traumatic event ... when suffering confounds us, we need to ask ourselves: whose feelings am I actually living?"[1]

Sometimes they are not our own. In fact, most of what we live out before we consciously work through our patterns is a direct result of what we've seen and experienced in our formative years. Unfortunately, my early childhood was marked by various forms of abuse ... incidents my subconscious was pretty good at reinforcing in me and drowning out simultaneously, until several decades later.

The brain can only repress memories for so long—and then, it leaks. This can result in erratic, confusing behaviors: lashing out, meltdowns, or if you're like me—illicit, immoral and illegal activity. Though it took me roughly five decades of trying unsuccessfully to suppress the mounting pain in my heart and head, I was fortunate enough to get to the

---

1   Wolynn, Mark. It Didn't Start with You. Viking Adult, 2017.

point where I would say *NO MORE* and get some real help for myself.

I met a specialist—an angel sent from heaven, who could hold the experiences I had that were extremely troubling. Kelly empowered me to recognize—*even though terrible things had been done to me ... I was not a victim.* I was invited to take radical responsibility for my behavior. While my wiring had made choices up to that point ... I was now fully cognizant of my patterns—this meant that *I was in control of my future ...* and there was no escaping the weight of that responsibility. Embracing the complete onus of myself and my life was the only way out.

Will Smith has a video called "Fault Versus Responsibility." In it, he talks about how we get to certain places in life due to the belief systems that we create. There, we meld our personas to our circumstances—responding and reacting *in character* to catalysts and influences. I call these masks *hidden identities*, which I cover in my courses.[2]

We create *hidden identities* when we assume roles and believe things about ourselves—for better and for worse—based on what we've seen, heard, or experienced and information we've adopted as *true* about our personalities.

These sides of our identities develop over time and while the positive aspects might work in our favor (when asking a girl out, or earning a big promotion), the negative ones can

---

2   Smith, Will, "Fault vs Responsibility". Instagram, 2018.

do major harm. While some serve us, some have no reason to exist. And yet, they do—and they impact us more than we realize.

The subconscious mind is powerful. Consequently, unexamined beliefs living beneath the surface can have a significant impact on our thoughts throughout life. Inevitably, these beliefs drive our everyday decisions, shape our emotional landscape and determine the actions we take—or do not take—in the pursuit of our goals. Often, we aren't able to identify them until they've negatively marked the trajectory of our lives. Without therapy, we might not see the strange ways we cope with emotions. The adoption of these identities is a result of how we perceive things that we've seen or things that have happened to us ... no matter how insignificant they may have appeared at the time. What we believe to be true for us is *true*.

The troubling reality about *parents* is that they are people. As such, they are fallible, imperfect and—like virtually every person alive—marked by trauma. Inevitably, humans inflict pain on other humans. *Hurt people hurt people*. In turn, parents pass down generational issues to their kids and their children's identities are shaped as a result.

In my case, it was both my parents' trauma being passed down to me and the pain inflicted by *other* children that constructed my inner world. Major, hurtful life events were amplified by *small* violations that continued throughout my high school years. These damages conditioned me to react in specific ways to the world around me. In turn, the culmination of these responses created my *hidden identities*. It wouldn't be until later that I would learn I was wholly in charge of who I was becoming.

In the video, Smith emphasizes that even though it's not our fault that we got to where we are, it is our responsibility to determine where we are going. No matter how long ago the problem was seeded inside of us, it has to be resolved and uprooted.

Smith says, "It's not somebody's fault if their dad was an abusive alcoholic, but it's for damn sure their responsibility to figure out how they are going to deal with those traumas and make a life out of it ... as long as we are pointing the finger—we are jammed and trapped in *victim mode*. When you are in *victim mode* you are suffering." When I heard this for the first time, it immediately reminded me of what Steve Frank, the head coach of my football team at Hamilton College, used to say: "Every time you point the finger at someone, there are three fingers pointing right back at you." He said it about 30 years ago, but it didn't really hit me until I watched Smith's video.[3]

This is a call to end the suffering ... by taking radical responsibility.

A lot of people don't want to take ownership of their lives because they are in a lot of pain. I empathize with that. As

---

3   Smith, Will, "Fault vs Responsibility". Instagram, 2018.

someone who has been debilitated by fear, depression and anxiety and in a hopeless prison of their own making—*quite literally*—I resonate with the emotions that come with facing the consequences of our actions (or our parents' choices). However, feelings are temporary. They can and should be felt and processed; allowing them to healthily move through our bodies keeps them from becoming long-term states. This means we do well to avoid letting helplessness, fear, sorrow and anger overwhelm us for prolonged periods of time, as they shape our inner narrative. These emotions add fodder to the victim mentality and before long, we're playing out old cycles of learned debilitation. In turn, we start blaming other people.

I too blamed other people ... for a very long time. Until it completely destroyed my life. Up until I lost everything for the fourth time, I couldn't recognize *blame* as a primary symptom of perceived victimhood. Whether it was the inflated blame of others or the exaggerated condemnation of myself, I was committed to a hopeless narrative that I'd created. It kept me feeling stifled, helpless, angry and stuck.

Inevitably, these emotional states kept me reeling—and perpetuating negative circumstances. I'm a big believer that our external lives reflect our internal realities. When we are fueled with negative emotions, it creates a disconnect between ourselves and the world. Our work ethic is impacted; our relationships suffer. In turn, we hurt others. We decide *people are against us* and that is the lens through which we see the behaviors of those in our inner circle.

As an unfortunate result, our loved ones can be giving us their best and we might not even see it. Then, we react irrationally—as though we've been forgotten, abandoned, or provoked. The receiver of our retaliatory behaviors sometimes responds by treating us kindly; but more often they respond by pulling away or severing ties, thus creating a self-fulfilling prophecy. When we assume the posture of the victim, we position others to be our aggressors. It's a role even the most innocent can be projected into ... which causes us *to lose*.

We sabotage relationships. We destroy opportunities. We repeat toxic patterns. And with each trip through this vicious circle of self-destruction, the outcomes—and the pain—get increasingly worse.

Because assuming the victim mentality keeps us in a disempowered place, our feelings stay hurt ... *all the time*. In addition to blame-laying, having chronic *hurt feelings* is a tell that we are not taking radical responsibility. In this position, we can find any reason to generate discontent ... in turn, we pout *a lot*. We can't handle it when other people are successful and we're not. This might sound like,

Why me?

Why them and not me?

Why, God, why?

We lose the ability to celebrate with others because we are lost in the mental space of feeling sorry for ourselves.

This fractures our ability to be genuine in our connections. In turn, our colleagues, friends and loved ones lose and *we lose*.

When we lend our attention to narratives fueled by envy, powerlessness, anxiety and discontent, we project our emotional landscapes onto the outside world. Not only does this negatively affect our ability to see reality clearly, but it also yields trauma reenactment.

A good example of this can be observed in how we experience rejection. Let's face it—rejection happens to all of us ... *and it sucks*. But we make it all the more challenging when we bring our past experiences into the present. If we were rejected by our parents as kids, the experience of losing a job, getting dumped, or being replaced on a project can hurt even worse. We interpret present rejection as personal when it's really a matter of perspective. By putting a negative narrative on these experiences, we take on the role of our little selves stuck in a cycle that is beyond our control. We project oppression on situations that might be neutral. We make people into bullies, bad guys and the villains of our story when we don't have to ... in fact, we could be using that energy to benefit ourselves elsewhere. But too often, we are stuck in a trauma loop and we cannot think rationally or make the diplomatic choice.

It's a basic confirmation bias. Rest assured—whatever you believe about a situation can alter the circumstance in and of itself. What we believe directly affects how we show up to engage with others. If we inhabit fear, reactivity, anger, or a past idea about how scenarios or people inherently *are*, we forfeit the opportunity to be present in the moment and see things in a balanced way. If I find myself or my clients set in an old belief ... where they are not even looking for an alternative answer, I challenge them to identify *a third way*. As humans, we like to make things binary—but nothing ever is. Those who have healed past their trauma will grow beyond black-and-white thinking and blame-laying; they will be able to enjoy experiences in a nuanced way. If you're ever caught between two choices, I challenge you to think of one more ... then another, then another. When we feel limited in possibilities, we are constraining ourselves to the victim mentality—most of defeating it is just finding a way to think ourselves upright.

Changing the Narrative

The human mind loves deficits ... they are the perfect places to write stories. Not only do we have a narrative-driven culture, but our brains are also wired to fill in the gaps when information is missing. This is an innate part of our survival. As infants, we make sense of the world by interpreting that which we do and do not see. If Mom is in sight, it means she is available to interpret and meet our needs. We feel comfortable ... because she is accessible. If Mom steps out of sight, we might take this to mean she is not accessible to meet our needs. We cry, knowing that makes her *come back* and care for us—and we find resolve.

Once we get older and learn to reason through multiple possibilities, the mom who isn't in front of us could be in a lot of places. We might picture her in the kitchen, in the garden, or running errands. The way we conduct ourselves as we search for her is directly correlated to *why* we need her and the stories we tell ourselves about where she is. If our story is one of helplessness ... we will experience distress until she returns. If our story is one of confidence ... we will be able to self-soothe, knowing *she'll be right back.* In every situation, our imaginative brains construct entire scenarios accounting for things we do not see—both positive and negative.

Later in life, this can work to our benefit—provided we have healthy self-esteem and are prone to assuming the best. But if our brains are rooted in victimhood or unhealthy thought patterns, we can be negatively influenced by reactivity and anxiety. When difficult emotions dictate how we show up in the world, consequences follow.

We all have that friend who is a chronic catastrophizer. The person who calls, frantically detailing an imagined worst-case scenario. He's *positive* that something terrible will come to fruition; so, he calls you up, and siphons *your* energy because he just can't reel it in!

As a result, you both waste valuable time on his crazed mental state–dialoguing for hours about things outside of his control. Your friend doesn't realize that the time he could spend addressing the problem is wasted worrying about the problem.

Additionally, his negative energy will inevitably go *somewhere*; infusing any situation with that kind of stress can make it devolve into something negative. The outcome might not be *exactly* what your friend's fearing—but it's definitely not going to create something great. I know this all too well because I was that friend for the better part of my life.

If we're lucky, we've met the alternative to the chronic catastrophizer. This is the person who has a strong sense of internal control. No matter how chaotic the circumstance, they maintain a sense of balance. They believe they are equipped to handle change, so when change comes (as it always does), they valiantly manage the outcome. These people are thoughtful, they don't make rash decisions, they don't get bowled over by fear because they are able to self-regulate and they are confident in their ability to cope. Everyone loves being around them because their self-assurance and authenticity give those around them energy and resolve. Their healthy inner narrative is evident because they carry themselves with abundant confidence. These are the people we should surround ourselves with and model ourselves after. They demonstrate radical responsibility and self-possession.

In my program, I help people take back their stories.

The process that got us to believe the way we presently do is the same process we can use to undo negative beliefs. To reprogram the wiring in our brain, we revisit the narratives we've told ourselves about our identities and circumstances since childhood. Then, we decide what we *want* to believe moving forward. We make thoughtful lists about our capabilities and balanced assessments about our points of growth. We take accountability for previous mistakes while showing ourselves radical compassion. We embrace that *we are loved and are worthy of love, as we are, where we stand, with nothing else to do.* We don't need anyone else's approval or acceptance, only our own. Once we come into agreement about this, we can champion ourselves in an entirely new way.

I'm disgusting.
I'm fat.
I'm useless.
I'm stuck.
I'm broken.
I'm not worthy.
It's hopeless.
It's impossible.
It's too hard.
It's over.

These are some of the lies that my narrative used to include.

Once they were fleshed out on paper and I could see the untruths sprawled across the page, I could acknowledge how much I was selling myself short. For many of my clients, these thoughts are so constant they don't even realize their prevalence. This results in chronic rumination and never-ending faultfinding.

Having identified the voice of my inner critic and his usual commentary ... I have come to a place of being able to slow these thoughts down and to respond to them.

~~I'm disgusting.~~	*I'm desirable.*
~~I'm fat.~~	*I'm beautiful.*
~~I'm useless.~~	*I'm valued.*
~~I'm helpless.~~	*I'm empowered.*
~~I'm broken.~~	*I'm under construction.*
~~I'm not worthy.~~	*I'm so very worthy.*
~~It's impossible.~~	*It's possible.*
~~It's too hard.~~	*It's manageable.*
~~It's hopeless.~~	*It's not over yet.*
~~I can't do it.~~	*I can do it.*

After mindfully working through this exercise for a consistent period of time, the negative thoughts dissipate significantly. While they may pop up occasionally, we're now in control of whether or not we let these negative demons wreak havoc on our sense of self and well-being. Remember, negative thoughts are normal; it's not about taking on more shame when they rear their ugly heads. Like any good method of healing, it's about integrating more of what serves us as opposed to removing what doesn't. I tell my clients, *never weed, overseed.* I'm no gardener ... but I love the concept. If weeds sprout up and overtake your flowerbed, no amount of uprooting them will solve your problems. But enough well-planted seeds can drive out their gnarly roots entirely. As we steward our minds—this principle stands.

No one cares about you, my inner narrative would say. It was a negative inner script that had started young. In part, it was due to living in a turbulent home. But the way the kids treated me at school just reiterated that this was true. Because my parents never cared to teach my siblings and me healthy parameters around eating, I struggled with my weight and was severely bullied. I had little to detract from my appearance because I was also lacking in the clothing department. Most of our clothes were gifted to us on special occasions like Christmas or the first day of school. I didn't have the flashiest sneakers, the most colorful school supplies, or the coolest toys. I only had my personality and after the age of 10 ... that really stopped working in my favor.

As a result, I would pander for people's attention, then be skeptical of them if they got too close. After winning their approval through being *the comedian* or people-pleasing ... I could never understand why they'd actually *picked me.* I assumed no one in their right mind would. After all, they weren't seeing the real me ... *Wally* was buried too far beneath the surface. So, I'd denigrate my worth with words that were negative, hurtful and disrespectful.

In my junior high school and high school years, I learned to make a joke of myself. I relayed the negative things I was thinking about myself verbally to the people around me. This would manipulate them into consoling me ... so that I could receive the attention I craved.

Self-deprecating humor was my primary form of communication. I was addicted to the heartful response of people who *just didn't want me to be so hard on myself.* I learned people were quick to say the opposite of whatever horrible point I was trying to make about myself. It got to a point where I was so addicted to the affirmation of others that I would see how far I could take my self-deprecation just to get attention.

I never realized how negatively this narrative was impacting me. When I started doing the work in my adult years, I became so cognizant of the pattern that I thought I didn't need to keep it in check. *If I can keep it in check when I'm doing it—I don't need to stop it!* I'd think.

Wrong.

While my dad rarely criticized himself verbally, he had no issue being hard on everyone else—I noticed a parallel pattern in his behaviors. The reality was ... virtually all of the Bresslers were significantly overweight at various times in their lives. My dad was an emotional eater—just like me. My parents' love for unhealthy food exacerbated his addiction of reaching for unhealthy foods when he was hungry. Every few years he'd meet with his doctor to learn he was *still* on a downward slope. So, he'd work with a dietician for a while, enjoy abrasively managing the diet of the entire household, then drop off the plan entirely—entering the same familiar cycle of self-sabotage.

I asked him once,

"Dad, why aren't you doing your diet anymore? You were doing so well! You lost like 15 pounds. Why did you stop?"

He said,

"It's the dietician's fault. She didn't follow up with me. I was doing what I was supposed to be doing. But it was their fault."

Their fault. Can you hear it? My dad's narrative about the entire situation was shaped by the victim mentality. Even though I could acknowledge its absurdity as a kid, I absorbed it. As an adult, I found myself blaming my issues with addiction on external circumstances.

And remember ... I absorbed my mom's patterns too ...

Wally! I can't believe you didn't call home! I thought you were in a ditch somewhere!

Walter. You need a job with insurance, benefits and a substantial paycheck.

We need to prepare for the worst.

We need to set ourselves up for success.

The bottom could fall out at any moment and remember ... good things never happen to us.

One would have thought my parents' fear-driven natures would have made them great with finances and in control of what they spent. But much like their unhealthy, binge-oriented eating cycle ... the opposite was true. Neither of them made an effort to equip themselves for success and their poverty mentality kept us in a state of being perpetually strapped for a long time.

Though Mom was one of the best educators in the state, Dad could barely hold down a minimum-wage job until he was finally hired on as a letter carrier in the early 80s. His dysfunction was that he would go as hard as possible in short stints, then burn himself out. Though we always had a roof over our heads and clothes on our backs ... I missed out on the things other kids had—and the layers of my parents' dysfunction facilitated the same dysfunction inside of me. It manifested the most with food.

It's funny how things stick in our memories because we make such a big deal of them at the time. I still remember the differences between the lunches that other kids had versus what I had each day. While all the other kids at school were enjoying Cow Tales—delicious, gooey caramels, snack cakes, chips, cookies—and even soda—with their lunches, Mom insisted *we just didn't have the money*. This created a deficit narrative with two parts for me: Finances and food. In these subtle ways, my mom passed her and Dad's poverty mindset on to me. Even today, I have to remind myself, *I deserve to have nice things*. Now, I see my desires through to heal the wound. This is how I take radical responsibility for my circumstances: Reparenting the parts of myself that need words to match actions. I tell myself a new story ... and then I follow through to bring my positive narrative into reality—this is all a significant part of the work of emotional healing.

There will come a time when journaling about our inner worlds is not enough. Once we establish what needs to change, we have to position ourselves to live out what we have come to believe. This means not just compulsively reading personal development books when our lives are in shambles; it also means keeping our word to ourselves when we start a new exercise regime, upholding healthy boundaries with colleagues who leech our time and energy and leaving unproductive relationships or circumstances when we know *it's time*.

It is impossible to heal until we are able to come through for ourselves in a real way. No one values unpredictability or people who make them feel fundamentally unsafe. It is our job—as the main characters of our stories—to demonstrate what we've learned through action. When we do, we tell our brains, *this is who we are now*. Before long, our new behaviors will be so second nature they will prove our new identity to be true.

Everything in Right Measure

My dad's sense of powerlessness manifested the most in his unrealistically high standards for other people. He was a perfectionist—in every sense of the word—and he imposed his unattainable expectations and moral philosophy on everyone around him. Some of this rigidity was a byproduct of having served in the military. He'd been a cook in the Air Force and his primary job was feeding those on active duty—save the times when there was a fatal accident and his role transitioned to helping scrape dead bodies off the tarmac. I always privately got a laugh out of that—and I mean *very* privately. Dad didn't have much of a sense of humor and if I ever made a joke around him, it was rarely met with a smile or a laugh.

Still, he once attempted to share this part of his life with me before totally ruining the moment. We woke up early to make the whole family breakfast. I stood, watching him carefully crack eggs on the side of the skillet, making sure no pieces of shell fell into the sizzling butter. He poured the yoke out evenly, let it solidify, then added in some vegetable slices and diced bacon from the cutting board. Then, he asked me if I wanted to try to fold the omelet. Eagerly, I agreed and he handed me the spatula. As I attempted to slide the thin part of the utensil beneath the egg, it caught and created a large hole that the toppings slipped through.

"Dammit, Wally!" he yelled, ripping the spatula out of my hand and shoving me out of the way. I stepped back, embarrassed—thinking I'd ruined everything.

"Dad, it doesn't have to be perfect ... " I offered, in an effort to redeem the moment. I instantly realized this was the wrong thing to say as his eyes widened with fury and he ferociously yelled back, "Yes it does!" Then he threw my omelet in the trash—an entire meal because it wasn't absolutely perfect.

Suffice it to say, I was traumatized by what could have been a bonding and teaching opportunity. I also lived the rest of my life being hypervigilant to perfectionism wherever it reared its ugly head. I see it in *many* of my clients. And it manifests in two ways: Over-execution on projects and the avoidance of work entirely. When everything has to be immaculate, priorities are hard to identify and nothing can be consistently *good*. After perfectionists reach a state of overwhelm (having taken far too much responsibility for everything around them), they shut down. That's when avoidance behaviors kick in. The smallest of messes or inconveniences can arise and their brains can't cope. *I'll take care of this tomorrow*, they tell themselves ... but tomorrow never comes. Tony Robbins summed up the ills of perfectionism best when he said,

People always try to be perfect. That's why they don't start anything. Perfection is the lowest standard in the world.

Because if you're trying to be perfect, you know you can't be.
So, what you really have is a standard you can never achieve.[4]

The way I manage perfectionism with my clients is by teaching them the concept of *everything in right measure*—we don't overdo taking on responsibility and we don't absolve ourselves of responsibility. It's about making progress in even the smallest increments, rather than being perfect. It requires knowing our stopping point and establishing internal boundaries and clear accountability with ourselves. This, paired with exercises that address shame, is what enables my avoiders to hop back into their workflow again. They stop procrastinating and embrace time management. They stop engaging in behaviors that *seem* important but aren't. They learn how to *just start*—because something decent is better than nothing. And the internal resistance of perfectionism can only be reprogrammed by a progression of small, deliberate, imperfect choices. Right measure is the only measure—this is your permission to *begin*.

A Healthy Sense of Control

Being a personal development coach is interesting because I assist people in cultivating a skill set that they should have learned from parents, teachers, coaches and other leaders

---

4   Robbins, Tony. "People Always Try to Be Perfect ... "

during their formative years—primarily the importance of boundaries and of establishing a healthy sense of mental and emotional control. In this life, there is very little we can dictate as far as outcomes go, but we can very much influence our circumstances by learning to manage our emotions, thoughts and perceptions.

Taking radical responsibility for our lives means *taking the reins* in every scenario ... regardless of how scary it may seem. Those who experience the world as a threatening place establish that narrative due to a lack of healthy boundaries. Their flimsy internal boundaries keep them in a state of people-pleasing—over-giving—to the point that they are taken advantage of, that they stay too long in situations that do not serve them and that they load more on their plate than they can manage—out of obligation.

There have been many instances in my life where I have given time, money and resources to others when I didn't have the means to afford it. On more occasions than I can count, I've lent emotional support to friends and acquaintances that should have been spent on myself and my family. Unfortunately, when we have low self-esteem and are boundaryless, we seek to *help others* to foster positive feelings about ourselves rather than dealing with our issues. The bad news is that when we ignore our own needs, care and desire for resolution, our problems worsen ... in the midst of helping others improve. We must care for ourselves before we can cater to the needs of others. The best metaphor I can think of is the *cabin pressure* portion of the safety talk that flight attendants give at the beginning of a flight:

> *In the event of a loss of cabin pressure, an oxygen mask will automatically appear in front of you. To start the flow of oxygen, pull the mask towards you. Place it firmly over your nose and mouth, secure the elastic band behind your head and breathe normally. Although the bag does not inflate, oxygen is flowing to the mask. If you are traveling with a child or someone who requires assistance, secure your mask first and then assist the other person.*

Left unchecked, these behaviors create chaos because none of them are appropriate or balanced. They yield resentment and shame, as well as emotional and physical exhaustion. Often, if internal boundaries are weak, external boundaries are not much stronger. We tell other people no but allow them to persuade us into a maybe. Time management is practically impossible because our stop and start times are too flexible. We let ourselves get roped into doing things that do not serve our schedule, energy, or enthusiasm because we do not know where we stop and where others begin. In turn, we spend our days entirely depleted and spread thin.

As I coach clients through accountability exercises that effectively help them keep their word *to themselves*, they start to recognize just how much they've taken on. When what we have to control is more centralized, we find that everything in life is more manageable. Our *yeses* and *nos* become harder, clearer and louder, because they enable us to be present and experience *living*. We are no longer tempted to add things to our mental, emotional, or professional load because we know those were all managing behaviors that we were exhibiting to keep us *safe*. The truth is, we are *already safe*, and have always been safe, inside ourselves.

Say it with me again. It won't be the last time you do.

I am not a victim.

Nowadays, I have a healthy sense of control. I know that I can self-regulate my emotions, manage my sleep schedule, take some time each day to exercise, work consistently without being distracted, not answer emails after a certain time and make sure that I do something great for myself as often as I can. I know who I am and I know where I end. I can teach these skills because establishing a routine was the first thing I did when I started therapy. Creating an agenda that worked for me made me feel empowered because my day had a sense of stability. It presented opportunities for me to be accountable to myself and tell myself *no*. In turn, I was able to build trust with myself ... something I'd never experienced in my adult life.

As I took back my internal narrative, I realized I could not be a hero *and* a victim. So, I took radical ownership of everything that was *mine* to steward ... and I built a brand-new life.

2

EMBRACING LITTLE ME

Putting on the Mask

For the most part, I've always been the biggest person in the room, even when I was very young. Physically and in my personhood—Little Wally and Big Wally have always *taken up space*. Over the decades, the measurements have looked different. When I was in elementary school, I was large. A bit taller than many of my classmates—and overweight. This, along with the fact that my clothes were poorly fitted and I rarely got anything new, only added to me feeling *less than* everyone else.

For as long as I can remember, I was big on the outside but shrinking on the inside—a byproduct of shame. This held true from first grade up until eighth grade. It was during this time that I learned I could cope with being made fun of if I could work *around* the punchline. So ... I became *the comedian—the wise guy*. Loud. Gregarious. Funny. Clever.

Quick-witted. And ... mischievous.

By the time third grade rolled around, I started getting into trouble. A lot of trouble. A culmination of *funny trouble* and *angry trouble*. In most instances, I thought I was just *being myself* ... but this newfound identity was shaped and fueled by the anger, pain and shame inside of me: An internal cycle I could not escape, due to my lack of ability to emotionally regulate.

To make matters worse, I received discipline and punishment at school in the same way I did at home. I was strongly disciplined whether I did something intentionally defiant—or unintentionally. Additionally, the punishment rarely fit the crime.

Once in third grade, I was checking out mentally in class, as I often did and I began twisting a pencil in my sweater to see how many revolutions I could make before there was no more give in the material. Upon the last twist of the pencil, my hand slipped and my sweater uncoiled like a snake striking its prey, shooting the projectile directly into my teacher's chest.

It wasn't on purpose. I wasn't trying to misbehave. Nobody got hurt. There was no malice intended. But there were also no questions asked about *why* or *how* it happened. My teacher looked at me with disgust, said nothing, then hastily pointed towards the door of the classroom—indicating that *it was time to go to the principal's office*. You would have thought I worked in the front office at Broad Street Elementary School for the amount of time I spent there either waiting for or meeting with the principal. The result of each visit was either a good chewing out or a repetitive, piercing poke to the chest—for emphasis—with each word of admonishment I received. I could literally feel my anger and shame grow and my self-esteem and self-worth shrink. In turn, the *poke to the chest* sensation became something I still physiologically feel when I experience shame.

What exacerbated each punishment was the fact that virtually every teacher and administrator in the Nashua, NH school system knew me. My mom started as a teacher there in 1967, the year before I was born. By the time I was in first grade, most of the educators at the schools in town knew my name. As such, with each incident of misbehavior, acting out, trying to be funny, goofing around, or legitimately causing trouble, my disdain for myself increased—because I was the *poorly behaved* child of a *well-respected* teacher. Because I didn't have the tools to modify my behavior or to relieve myself of the inner turmoil I was experiencing, it became a vicious cycle of self-destruction that only got worse as time went on.

Many self-help books talk about the roles we assume as kids if we grew up in homes with abusers or addicts: *The scapegoat, the helper, the comedian, the hero, the golden child and the black sheep.* There are several more and varying pieces of literature that break out the unique details of each role. The general consensus is that we can be a culmination of more than one role at any given time, though one will be the most prevalent throughout our lives. Little Wally's baseline was *the lost child*, but that evolved into a combination of *the comedian, the hero* and later ... *the black sheep.*

Big Wally's cocktail of personality traits (for better and for worse) was largely due to nurture. The most terrifying part of therapy was not wondering *why I was the way I was*, but rather—wondering if I would have ever become *the way I was* ... if I hadn't been forced to mask my identity.

It's called a *sales persona* for a reason. We are usually the ex-class clowns, the extroverts, the performers, the chronic over-sharers and the over-zealous. My more reserved and introverted clients don't always know what to make of my impassioned approach to sales and my courses. Here's this guy with a booming laugh, a boisterous sense of humor, a direct approach and a desire to succeed at any cost. Not to mention the fact that the whole *used car salesman* stereotype doesn't bode well with most (a stereotype that I would argue exists for a reason—due to the *unhealed* personalities in the industry that exacerbate it). But, by the end of our work together, my clients gain a better understanding of *why* I am the way I am and *how* I've come into a full embrace of myself: The healthy parts and the parts that still need work.

As I've learned to celebrate my *large* identity, shaped by my triumphs and my traumas—I'm far less insecure about my appearance. And that's not to say I don't still struggle with emotional eating. *I do.* But I can identify my triggers and patterns when I'm in the midst of emotional distress and if I go on a bender ... I can be patient with my wounded parts while I choose self-compassion.

I am not naive enough to believe I am immune to the issues that deeply affected Little Wally. Low self-esteem and a lack of impulse control dictated my experience from a very young age. Financial deprivation resulted in my hoarding food and scrounging any snacks anytime I could find them, inside or outside my house.

When I was very young, as early as three years old, a common punishment I received was to be sent to bed without dinner. This routine disciplinary strategy created in me a fear of being hungry and not being able to access food. By the time I was six years old, I had become a full-on compulsive eater. My first recollection of binge eating was my first day of first grade. It was snack time and the student who went to collect the crate of milk cartons from the cafeteria was handing them out to the other students in the class. As the other kids enjoyed a small snack and their milk, I opened up my *Kung Fu* lunch box and proceeded to eat my entire lunch. I was so afraid I would *go without* that I ate the whole thing—including my morning snack—without giving it a second thought. My preoccupation with consumption did not stop with food. It was with anything that created a *numbing out* experience.

I'd get home and park in front of the television until my parents came home from work—digesting cartoons constantly, just so I didn't have to think about my home life. This habit devolved into a darker vice after I experienced something no child should have to shoulder.

When I was 10 years old, I was molested by an extended family member. It was such a confusing, static, foreign experience that my brain could not process it. Though I was violated, I didn't *feel* violated ... I didn't feel anything at all. My survival mind compartmentalized the trauma of the incident—and the pain of it did not surface until I was fully grown.

Instead of indicating that something *wasn't right*—my body started craving sex. I discovered pornography in the form of the adult magazines in my dad's top drawer and I got so lost and isolated in it before puberty ... my parents would have had a hard time helping me even if that was their intention.

But it was never their intention.

My parents never talked about sex with me. Nor did they teach me how to protect myself from others. They never said to me, *Do not touch other people's bodies and don't let other people touch yours. And if someone does, please come tell us.* It was as if sex and intimacy didn't exist.

My *sex talk* with my dad was comical and sad at the same time. One Saturday afternoon when I was 12, my dad called me into the kitchen because he needed to talk to me. As I entered the kitchen, I saw one of his adult magazines on the kitchen table. I immediately panicked, thinking I was about to get the punishment of all punishments because he'd discovered that I had been looking at his magazines. Instead, he sat me down and opened a centerfold of a naked woman right there in front of me.

This is what sex is, he said—explaining very little. *Just be careful and always ask permission.* The whole time, all I could think was how shocked and disappointed he would be to know that I'd looked at and pleasured myself to that very same picture dozens of times over the last couple of years.

And that was it.

In fourth grade, I was sexually abused.

In fifth grade, I was compulsively looking at pornography magazines.

By sixth grade, I was having sex on a regular basis.

And no one even saw—because out of all my budding addictions—that there was one that trumped them all ...

I was a phenomenal, fantastical, habitual *liar*.

***

In the ninth grade, I had one significant experience of an adult actually caring about me. I tried out for the football team and made the cut. I figured I'd be popular in no time if I followed my coach's guidance about lifting weights. So, I hit the gym. I began exercising in the way I still begin things—I went hard. I drank a lot of water, followed an eating plan and was sweating it out to be a better football player. When I started dropping weight, I felt really good about myself and even my dad agreed I looked better. But when the season ended, I followed my dad's logic on my fitness regime.

My coach didn't keep checking up on me—so I forfeited my follow-through.

Instead of training, I spent the summer watching my parents try *yet again* to lose weight together—as it became more evident that the Bressler family tradition was to never finish *anything* we started.

Enter Weight Watchers. It's unreal to me that gimmicky programs like Jenny Craig and the points system have thrived all these years, but it's pastel-wearing women like *my mom* who have kept them in business. On the occasions when my parents wanted to be health-conscious, they would take action to get the ball rolling. My mom signed herself and me up for Weight Watchers more than a few times.

Picture young, chubby Wally—sitting between Karen and Susan with his points diary while they cried about the results of their weigh-in. I could only take it seriously for so long. I'd keep to the points system for a while, but unsupervised—I'd paw at Mom's high-point desserts in the freezer, then end up restricting myself to four treats per day. By night, I'd be starving, so I'd down all of the leftovers from dinner— convincing myself I'd *get back on track* tomorrow, which would prove to be exactly the same.

We tried many diets and they helped temporarily with the deprivation cycle. But in the end, it didn't matter, because we never fully committed to making them work.

I felt isolated at school, even resentful, because other kids had all kinds of things in their lunchboxes. Rice crispy treats. Twinkies. Small boxes of Trix. I'd hide my apple and evenly measured stack of Melba toasts so that my classmates wouldn't make fun of me for being on a diet. No matter how I tried to escape it, everything pointed back to my weight issues—the physical manifestation of my much deeper troubles.

In the 80s, the cultural conversation on trauma wasn't a thing. Research on weight loss did not yet emphasize what we would later discover: *It's all in your head.* Our relationship with food is 100% psychological. Mine was a byproduct of my parents' inability to adequately care for me ... and for themselves.

In turn, the entire Bressler family suffered from low self-esteem. We were just determined to hide it. A mark of the era was that only *crazy* people—only people with *real* issues—went to therapy. Up until the day my mom died of lung cancer from being unable to quit smoking roughly 45 years—she never set foot in a therapist's office.

Life back then was about portraying an illusion in which your picture-perfect family was *more* than OK. But beneath the surface, our family was eroding with generational trauma, secrets and blatant lies. It was the culmination of these things that compromised *both* my parents' quality of life and their happiness. They, like so many other families at that time, cared more about public opinion than about getting the help they needed—so, they forfeited removing the mask that was costing us our sanity.

The Defiant Walter Bressler

At the age of 10 years old, I became public enemy number one of my elementary school. I was a true menace— the *Defiant Walter Bressler* who lied habitually and both verbally and physically fought kids in school. I was angry. Communicating using my furious verbal assaults and even my fists, was the only way I could get the anguish out. I could only hold in my anger for so long until I exploded— punching kids in the face, tripping them as they stepped off the school bus, kicking people when they weren't looking and even throwing rocks at them. When my knuckles would meet flesh, every face I swung at was a representation of the words my dad had said to me, words that had marked my identity and wounded my heart.

What's interesting is that my parents never taught me to protect myself in fights, so I would take a tremendous amount of verbal and physical abuse until I couldn't take it anymore. One time, they came up with the money to get me karate lessons in an effort to help me develop some discipline and skills to defend myself—*gi* and white belt included.

Unfortunately, once they dropped me off at class, I waited for them to leave, then went across the parking lot to the bowling alley to eat candy and play video games. They never asked how class went, or if I'd learned anything. So, I got away sneaking and binging on treats throughout that 90-day training period.

Consequently, I improved neither my level of discipline nor my skills in protecting myself. In turn, I continued with my ineffective strategies of self-defense: I would fight back using words first—then fists after I'd reached my boiling point. I became an emotional stuffer and a coward ... and I'd remain a coward for the next four decades, letting people take advantage of and walk all over me.

In the midst of this, I'd grown contemptuous toward my dad over the years—developing an ambivalence to his physical violence and unreasonable punishments. After so many nights of being sent to bed without dinner, anger filled the spot in my stomach where food should have been. My feelings oscillated between adrenaline rushes and a tingling, numb, slow-motion sensation. By that point, it'd happened too many times—being confined to the isolation of my own bedroom in ways that communicated aggression and contempt, but never healthy discipline.

Dad's scary discipline tactics continued throughout my childhood. At my ninth birthday party, Mom had planned a big event at the house. The backyard was set up with games for kids to play. There was a gift table covered in presents from other children—something that made me elated, as I only received minimal and practical gifts from my parents and family members. I eyed the glossy, brightly colored packages, then noticed the snack table complete with a birthday cake that read *Happy Birthday, Walter!* And all around me were kids ... kids who liked me, who wanted to play with me, who were there to celebrate me for my special day.

Then, the worst possible thing happened. I made a joke—*an innocent*, ignorant joke, about my dad's weight. His face immediately hardened and despite the other adults standing around, he grabbed my arm with force and proceeded to drag me into the bathroom.

"You're done here," he said, yanking my party hat off.

He put me to bed at 2 p.m. on a sunny July afternoon. I sat and watched from my bedroom window while the other kids played for the rest of the afternoon—celebrating my birthday without me. I kept thinking Mom would come and knock on my door to soften the situation—invite me back outside to open all my presents. But she never came for me. No one came for me, until the next morning ... when Dad finally opened the door, reiterated his point, then exited with a seriousness that made me feel like I was still in trouble. He was treated harshly himself as a child and was the king of the silent treatment. He never helped me establish mental peace or emotional resolve after a fight; he liked keeping the control in his hands.

After years of handling every behavioral *incident* with callousness ... I decided the crime should start fitting the punishment. I figured if I was going to be in trouble either way, I might as well make it worth the repercussions.

***

One of the more significant, defiant, *creative* acts of my childhood was a collaborative effort—with my female friend who lived next door to me. For me, it was difficult to make friends—so getting attention from someone—especially *a girl*—was a really, really big deal. Anne and I had played outside for most of the day and had been tinkering around in my dad's shed when we found a gallon of gray house paint near his workbench, complete with paint brushes that were three times the size of our hands.

"Let's play like we're painters, Walter!" Anne exclaimed. I agreed with complete, *dumb* enthusiasm—not fully understanding what her idea entailed.

"Well, come on!" she said, motioning for me to help her with the paint supplies—gesturing that I follow her back to her house. While she carried the paintbrushes, I hoisted up the heavy bucket and followed her next door ... in broad daylight, mind you.

There, we decided to give a little *facelift* to the side of her house. The longer we painted, the more enthusiastic we became. We'd step back, admire our work and keep going.

Right around sunset, a familiar car cruised down the block in front of Anne's house. Her dad's white four-door rolled into its usual parking space as Anne peeked around the side of the house—making direct eye contact with her father. Everything after that happened quickly. Her dad stepped out of the car, aghast.

There were loud expletives and flabbergasted sighs as he put his hand over his eyes. Within minutes Anne's mom joined him, saying nothing ... standing in complete silence and shock ... wondering how we'd covered so much area with so little paint.

I could see the look of distress on Anne's face, a look that indicated she'd never been in that much trouble before. And then I was gripped with fear ... *would I be in trouble, too?*

"Get your things, Walter. I'm going to have a talk with your father," Anne's dad said.

I swallowed hard and all the blood left my face as I looked into my own driveway to see that my dad was indeed home. Inside our house, my parents were probably sitting on the couch smoking cigarettes—watching television, hoping not to be bothered.

Within a matter of minutes, my dad's temper would flash from zero to bloodcurdling rage. I anticipated his wrath would be similar to things I'd experienced in the past. But this time—he took his rage out on me more violently than he ever had.

If you've ever been hit by a leather belt, you are very familiar with the marked swooshing sound that happens as the belt is being rapidly removed from the belt loops that keep it in place. Because it was the '70s and polyester was a prominent material for clothing, the swooshing sound was very noticeable—warning you of your impending punishment.

As I lay across Mom and Dad's bed with my bare backside exposed—he whipped me with his belt so hard it left large welts across my skin. It hurt to sit for at least a day or two. What was even more painful was the fact that I was also grounded for at least a month. I'd come home, go to my room and shut the door. There—I didn't have anything but my own thoughts to keep me occupied.

Left isolated, with neither guidance nor comfort, my contempt toward my parents only grew. By the time I was *released* from my punishment, I felt like an animal coming out of its cage and I dove headfirst into the things that had always brought me relief: Food, pornography and lying about mischievous behavior.

The cycle my dad sought to break with negative reinforcement was only exacerbated. Under their own roof of staunch discipline where I was being watched like a hawk—my parents' efforts to reel me in were proving to be counterproductive. Then, Little Wally started to spin completely *out of control*.

The Wounds of Little Wally

My dad's stern disciplinary tactics were also meted out to my siblings—a direct result of his upbringing and inextinguishable anger that kept him hostile on a fairly regular basis. He'd been raised by Mimi and Poppy. Mimi was an angry Sicilian woman whose great-grandparents had immigrated to the United States. She lived her life with a chip on her shoulder, a scowl on her face and no moral philosophy whatsoever.

Her mouth was full of racist epithets and unkind words about others. Those weren't things Mom or Dad would ever say—my dad had been scarred for life by his mother's hatred. Toward others. Toward him. Mimi was particularly evil toward Poppy. Because he was the weaker one out of the two, he was complicit, as Mimi was a tyrannical disciplinarian toward my dad, ultimately molding him to be an unhappy and often angry person.

Mimi had a penchant for scapegoating people. If she was feeling antagonistic, she'd make up an accusation, ask Dad and my aunt repeatedly if they'd done something wrong, then when they'd deny the accusation—she'd beat them.

This taught both of them to falsely admit to guilt— thereby conceding to a lesser form of punishment. Dad in particular, as Mimi had grown so infuriated with him once that she had thrown him off the back deck of their house for not completing a task she had asked him to take care of. This left a noticeable scar on my dad's chin and countenance ... something I had never observed in detail until he was lying in his casket that afternoon in early December 1991.

Despite having an unfortunate upbringing, Dad never showed signs of weakness. He'd learned to never become that vulnerable with family. His inner childhood wounds kept him from being able to properly relate to his children, an issue that never found resolution before he finally, symbolically, died of significant *heart issues*.

Heart and *mind* issues marked the Bressler family—and no one dared to talk about it. On one of the most traumatic occasions of my childhood, I awoke in the middle of the night to commotion in the kitchen while Grandpa, Grandma, and Aunt Pat, my mom's father, mother and sister respectively, were visiting. I made my way down the dark hallway to the kitchen following frantic, overlapping voices.

There, on the linoleum floor, my father's sister was performing CPR on my Grandma. Grandpa paced nearby, rotary wall phone in hand, speaking with the 911 operator. Grandma was having a stroke. I stood in the doorway, frozen and stunned. When the flashing lights of the ambulance arrived, everyone chased the gurney out.

After a few harrowing days in the hospital, Grandma *was not in the best shape*. She ended up getting placed in a rehabilitation facility, where we would visit her regularly until she died at a fairly young age. The unfortunate thing is that no one ever spoke about what happened that night with me. Neither my mom nor my dad sat down to process the incident with their 10-year-old son. It was as if it'd never happened *at all*.

Though Mom grew up in a low-income, blue-collar home—she was not raised in an atmosphere with the same emotional deficit as my dad. What her parents lacked financially, they compensated for in love. Her parents were humble people. My grandfather immigrated from Italy when he was a little boy and my grandmother grew up in the modest suburbs of West Virginia. Later in life, they made their way to Brooklyn, where they met idyllically at Ebbets Field during a Brooklyn Dodgers game when one of them turned to the other and asked for a cigarette. Who asked who is still unknown today.

Baseball was my grandfather's whole life; he'd travel the country just to keep up with his team. Though he hadn't even finished high school, he had a decent work ethic and was fueled by the belief that one should *work to live*, not *live to work*. When he was single, he had a knack for landing gig jobs and centered his whole life around following the Brooklyn Dodgers wherever they were playing. It was just enough to keep him on his feet throughout the season. After he married my grandmother, he spent a good portion of his adult life working at the hospital where I was born.

Grandma stopped him on the Dodger's home turf that year and stilled his interest in traveling. They bonded over the love of the game ... and smoking cigarettes—a tragic irony in retrospect.

They never had much in the way of money, but they did what they had to do to make ends meet. In addition to working at the meat counter in the local grocery store, Grandma also loved wrapping presents at Macy's in New York City during Christmas. She was good at gifts, even if she wasn't the one giving them. She enjoyed the way the paper felt beneath her hands, perfecting the lines of every crease and tucking translucent pieces of tape out of sight. That was the symbol of someone's holiday in her hands—a commemoration of family.

So, she took it seriously, even though *Christmas* had a different bent in our family entirely. For us, there was less of an emphasis on the commercial pageantry of the holiday and more of an emphasis on the liturgical traditions of the Roman Catholic Church and the Italian customs that went with it.

As much of a headache as it is to explain ... *we were Catholic*. With apologies to those of you who are Catholics, anyone who is not raised Catholic will never understand what a pain in the ass it is to be Catholic. Moreover—we were Roman Catholics. So ... we were the louder, gaudier, more *involved* kind during the holidays.

Christmas Eve is big for Italians. We'd celebrate the Feast of the Seven Fishes each year with an array of fish options and obviously other things that weren't fish. We'd have trays of cheese and marinated vegetables, loaves upon loaves of Italian bread with lots of butter available for spreading, a sweets table, baskets of fruits and nuts and coolers full of soda and beer. I loved every minute of that day as it meant there was a lot of great-tasting food and I could eat as much as I wanted to. It was *an event.*

No one in my family had much money, but I could count on the basics: Socks, shoes, underwear and books. One Christmas, Dad splurged on the most meaningful gift of my childhood ... it was one thing I'd really wanted, but I'd never imagined we could afford it. An electric Snoopy toothbrush. He gave it to me before he headed out to work his managerial night shift at Burger King on Christmas Eve. It was the greatest thing I'd ever gotten ... something I needed *and* wanted—that made me wonder if my dad loved me *after all.*

***

In the years prior to being sent to my bedroom as a punishment, there was the corner. I spent most of my early childhood in some sort of a timeout. Sitting. Waiting. Thinking. Namely about how bad I was. To pass the time, I'd stare at our popcorn ceiling—looking for shapes in it. I'd count as high as I could ... but I wasn't old enough to get to 100 and I didn't even know the alphabet yet. Other times, when I would act out or be *fresh*, I would get my mouth washed out with soap or caked red hot pepper flakes, with no water to cleanse my palate until the punishment was considered sufficient. In turn, I used hot pepper flakes on my children's tongues when they were younger and I regret doing it to this day.

My time spent being disciplined in isolation was restless, but it beat the alternative of being swatted with Mom's wooden spoon, a shoe, or whatever was closest for her to grab. I learned to stop talking back and not wiggle too much. The repercussions weren't worth the struggle. So, I complied.

I memorized the smell of the corner—I'd press my nose up to the wall, catch a waft of flat white paint paired with the dusty smell of old carpet that sat right outside of foot traffic. It was a lonely place, where my stomach clenched and my jaw muscles tightened from grinding my teeth.

When I'd finally be allowed out of the corner, I'd have such a bad headache, I'd want to go and lie down. I'd hear my dad's words spinning in my head—my small body shaking from how loud he'd yelled things like,

You're done here.
You're bad.
You've lost your chance.
You're worthless.
It's over for you.

Dad's dense approach to punishment was abrupt and his words about my identity and how I'd messed up things with my innocuous mistakes made me chronically anxious. Not only was Little Wally covered by shame ... he was taught that the smallest error could ruin an entire shopping trip, birthday, holiday, or family vacation. I didn't have the ability to distinguish that it was my dad's disproportionate reaction to my behavior that was keeping everyone on eggshells, as opposed to my behavior itself. This was the most confusing when I'd only done something to annoy Dad—and had not really broken the rules at all.

As a result, my brain learned that—despite my best intentions and ignorance ... I could be doing something horribly wrong and not even be aware of it. And even if I was doing everything to Dad's standards, it didn't matter ... because there was still something fundamentally wrong with me. In turn, my dad's outer critic became the voice of my internal antagonist, who kept me confined to the corner for many years—even in my most accomplished moments.

**

For thrivers of complex trauma, Pete Walker's material is canon. In both *The Tao of Fully Feeling* and *Complex PTSD: From Surviving to Thriving*, Walker writes on the importance of re-parenting and teaching our inner children to emotionally regulate. Leading research on somatic healing methods shows that repression stems from our desire to avoid the physical sensations of emotion. Walker notes,

There is often a close relationship between emotion and physical

sensation. Physical sensations in the body often co-occur with feelings. Moreover, sensations of tightness and tension can develop as a defense against feelings. As unexpressed feelings accumulate, a greater degree of muscular tension is necessary to keep them under wraps. A child who is repeatedly punished for emoting learns to be afraid of inner emotional experience and tightens [armors] the musculature of her body in an effort to hold feelings in and to banish them from awareness. Holding your breath is a further manifestation of armoring. It is an especially common way of keeping feelings at bay, as breathing naturally brings your awareness down to the level of feeling.[5]

Those who struggle with addiction of any form in adulthood usually do so to temper the physical sensations that accompany difficult emotions that they were not able to process during childhood. Emotions like shame, anxiety and anger can catalyze what Walker refers to as *emotional flashbacks*. If a child was severely neglected, but every time they were neglected, they found comfort in pantry snacks— an emotion like loneliness will trigger the craving for a salty, sweet form of relief every time their adult self is triggered.[6]

Part of re-parenting our inner children involves learning

---

5   Walker, Pete. *PTSD: From Surviving to Thriving: A Guide and Map For Recovering from Childhood Trauma.* Azure Coyote, 2013.
6   Walker, Pete. *PTSD: From Surviving to Thriving: A Guide and Map For Recovering from Childhood Trauma. Azure Coyote,* 2013.

our most triggering emotions, tracing them to their earliest occurrence or an identifiable pattern, then speaking to ourselves with the affirmation and compassion we didn't receive as children around those memories. Establishing the ability to emotionally regulate builds new pathways in our brains (habits) that re-establish our baseline emotion. In turn, we no longer need old coping strategies to survive. We can hold our attachments, vices and false identities more loosely ... until we are willingly able to release them.

When it comes to healing the wounds of our inner children, unconditional love and self-compassion is the ultimate remedy. And with this love, consistency is key. This is why it's beneficial to work with a therapist or coach while healing from childhood neglect or abuse. If we do not prioritize affirmation and self-soothing every time we feel ourselves slipping—we reinforce the intermittent love patterns that were demonstrated to us by our parents.

Walker notes,

Contempt is extremely traumatizing to a child and at best, extremely noxious to an adult. Contempt is a toxic cocktail of verbal and emotional abuse, a deadly amalgam of denigration, rage and disgust. Rage creates fear and disgust creates shame in the child in a way that soon teaches her to refrain from crying out, from ever asking for attention. Before long, the child gives up on seeking any kind of help or connection at all. The child's bid for bonding and acceptance is thwarted and she is left to suffer in the frightened despair of abandonment. Particularly abusive parents deepen the abandonment trauma by linking corporal punishment with contempt. Slaveholders and prison guards typically use contempt and scorn to destroy their victims' self-esteem. Slaves, prisoners and children, who are made to feel worthless and powerless devolve into learned helplessness and can be controlled with far less energy and attention. Cult leaders also use contempt to shrink their followers into absolute submission after luring them in with brief phases of fake unconditional love.[7]

Because fake unconditional love is a key part of the abuse cycle, it is integral to our healing that self-affirmation comes from an authentic place. Internal affirmation must have substance. It's more than repetition, sticky notes, popular anecdotes and mantras. Committing to our own healing means committing ourselves to an internal narrative of self-compassion. If the conversation we keep having with ourselves is full of correctives—it does not serve us. Moreover, it's usually a regurgitated script handed down from our caregivers. In his work, Walker emphasizes the two ways criticism manifests in abuse survivors: Internally or externally. Depending on how the child's psyche learned to defend their ego—the critic established its audience.

---

7   Walker, Pete. *PTSD: From Surviving to Thriving: A Guide and Map For Recovering from Childhood Trauma.* Azure Coyote, 2013.

When I first started therapy, I had no idea how to run off of positive reinforcement. Having grown up in an environment that stressed messages like *get good grades or get punished*—going easier on myself felt ... counterproductive. I had to contend with a new question that I could not shake— can I be nice to myself and also succeed?

I'll admit—the high of the sales profession can become an addiction in itself and much of my work has been pursuing the industry from a healthy perspective. You'd be surprised to know that the clients I experience the most concern over are not the ones who have an acknowledged issue with picking up the phone and making their calls; instead, I lose sleep at night over the ones with Jerry Maguire energy. They are hyped. They are manic. They are ready to win. They are careening. They are about to crash at any given moment, due to their fragile egos. These are the clients with the most irritable inner critics. They act like volatile, reactive, petulant children—because they are. A sales peak gives them too much of a positive hit. One great call and they are launched into unsustainable elation that will inevitably lead to a crash when the bottom falls out (and the bottom will fall out in sales—it's the nature of the industry).

The lows for Jerry Maguire's clients lead to terrifying ends: Long periods of time where they can't get out of bed, pursuing any means of escape, dissolving relationships with the rest of their book of business due to a lack of care, filing bankruptcy because they've tanked their finances, or giving way to patterns of self-harm and suicidal tendencies. This happens for two reasons: Not only have they allowed their successes and fears to become their identity—they have a ruthless inner narrative driving home what a worthless piece of junk they are if they don't succeed. And trust me ... without my personal commitment to introspection, rewriting my internal narrative and self-compassion—I would never have been able to heal the very prevalent Jerry Maguire energy inside of myself.

According to Dr. Kristin Neff, author of *Self-Compassion: The Proven Power of Being Kind to Yourself*, there are three components of self-compassion:

1.Self-Kindness vs. Self-Judgment
2.Common Humanity vs. Isolation
3.Mindfulness vs. Overidentification

Neff addresses the importance of absolving the inner critic when we are feeling the most vulnerable, instead of toughening up, pushing through, or addressing internal wounds with a "no pain no gain" approach. Because of the separateness children of abuse experience in childhood, Neff notes their propensity to self-isolate in her second point. Whether it's because they learned to build an internal world that didn't take into consideration the experiences of others or because they feel that isolation is the only thing they deserve—it is common for traumatized adults to think, "why me?" as opposed to focusing on the collective "we." We all experience pain. Because pain can be a great unifier ... shifting the narrative to "I am not alone in this" can be deeply healing. Finally, Neff encourages trauma thrivers to choose mindfulness when trying to break the pattern of overidentification with negative thoughts.[8] In my adult years, healing Little Wally looked like choosing to breathe, center and meditate when I'd hear my dad's script in my head. Instead of focusing on,

You're done here.
You're bad.
You've lost your chance.
You're worthless.
It's over for you.

I learned to focus on getting centered instead. Once my physiology was more balanced, I could address the unproductive thoughts that still spun in my adult head.

You're done here.	*You're safe here.*
You're bad.	*You're human.*
You've lost your chance.	*There's always one more chance.*
You're worthless.	*You're worthy.*
It's over for you.	*The best is yet to come.*

---

8   Neff, Kristin. *Self-Compassion.* HarperCollins e-books, 2011.

Seeing Is Believing

In our formative years, we look to our parents to teach us about the world and how we fit into it. Up until the age of eight, our sense of identity is shaped by the way our parents respond to us. Ultimately, they are the mirrors in which we find our reflection. Their verbal opinions and responses to us (or lack thereof) condition us to believe specific things about ourselves. For every child, these messages are different. In addition to characterizations about our personality and identity—we learn the rules of surviving in the world based on our parents' disciplining patterns. For Little Wally, staying alive meant accepting,

> *Approval is earned through good behavior.*
> *Showing emotions is weak.*
> *Taking risks leads to negative consequences.*
> *Nourishment is dependent on obedience.*
> *There is no room for error—life is unforgiving.*
> *Consumption, of any kind, can ease the pain.*

As a child, I bought into my parents' opinions about me and their feelings and beliefs about the world. My dad lived by the common adage, *truth hurts*. His implication was that everyone in our family should just absorb the blunt-force trauma of anything he deemed to be true at the moment.

There was no such thing as subjective truth in our family—no room for nuance. There was Dad's word alone. Its finality left little room for my siblings and me to examine our own beliefs, so we carried his truth until either it destroyed us or we gained the courage to choose better for ourselves.

One of the primary things I tell my clients is that we must learn to esteem the value of total honesty as opposed to brutal honesty. When there is no emotional safety around the delivery of truth, it cannot be told in love and if truth is not told in absolute love and with the highest consideration of the receiver's wellbeing ... it is not the full truth. For every negative fact about ourselves ... there is a well-rounded truth. We all have our blind spots. And we need healthy people in our lives to call out the deficits in us, but only within the parameters of healthy connection.

We don't have to metabolize every harsh thing someone says about us—especially if there's only a fraction of truth in it. A broken mirror, a convex mirror, a concave mirror ... is still a mirror. It is our responsibility as healing adults to be selective about the mirrors we allow into our lives, because ... seeing is believing.

Now that we are adults, we get to play gatekeeper to what we experience; the things we see and believe have to do largely with our ability to walk away when a relationship dynamic influences us to feel terrible about ourselves. Healthy relationships entail honest feedback; healthy feedback consists of total honesty and grace. We've been taught to believe that if we don't take it on the chin, if we receive the truth without tact—it means something about us. When in fact, pursuing health means holding the things others say about us loosely and examining statements with unrelenting grace for ourselves.

Sure. What they said might have been factual. But it's not a reflection of my identity or level of worthiness as a person. It might be true. But it is not the full truth. I think Abraham Maslow was on to something when he said we need to "Be independent of the good opinion of other people."[9]

Dr. Robert Stern, author of *The Gaslight Effect: How to Spot and Survive the Hidden Manipulations Others Use to Control Your Life,* suggests the following parameters when considering feedback: "You should never listen to criticism that is primarily intended to wound, even if it contains more than one grain of truth."[10]

Stern goes on to demonstrate how those with manipulative behavioral patterns—primarily individuals with cluster B personality traits, damage their victims with the misuse and abuse of truth. He details how this is a major component of gaslighting—the now popular term defined by Stern in 2007 as the act of undermining another person's reality by denying facts, the environment around them, or their feelings.

9   Maslow, Abraham H., and Robert Frager. *Motivation and Personality.* New Delhi: Pearson Education, 1987.
10 Stern, Robin. *The Gaslight Effect.* Harmony, 2018.

The benefit of Stern's research is that it discourages readers from diagnosing others and places responsibility on his audience to identify relational dynamics that result in them feeling triggered, depressed, or outright sick.[11]

Because seeing is believing, it is up to us to live in integrity when assessing ourselves and when evaluating other people who are positioned to speak into our lives. Being able to heal Big Wally was directly tied to my healing the unhealthy things Little Wally was taught to see in himself. As I learned how to overturn every stone of myself, I came to find ... I liked myself. I mean ... I authentically enjoyed the characteristics about myself that made me Wally. I knew I was seeing myself more clearly when I started craving time alone, just to get to know myself better. My ingrained contempt toward Little Wally slowly transformed into deliberate acceptance and thereafter ... consistent love, that continually sheds its conditions as I age. I am no longer tormented by the mistakes of Big Wally.

In fact, I enjoy his character development. He's the type of guy who will love you into the ground and who always has the best jokes. I'd laugh with him, grab a beer with him and cry with him. It took decades, but he's become my favorite hero, because even though he is tragic, he has a hell of a character arc. Wally Bressler is the type of hero who has

---

11 Stern, Robin. *The Gaslight Effect*. Harmony, 2018.

been down and out, who has made big mistakes and who has certainly fallen from grace …

But no matter how incomprehensibly bleak circumstances have been—He always gets back up again.

3

HEROIC GRIEF

What Happened to You?

One of the reasons clients come to me for coaching is that they realize their personal life is intertwined with their approach to sales and business. Their decision to take radical responsibility for their lives and work puts them in a position to release the victim mentality and learn the steps I've outlined in my *Phone Sale Secrets* courses and workshops. What they fail to recognize is that building a solid professional foundation is solely contingent on the solidity of the foundation we have inside ourselves. Ever heard the saying *a chain is as strong as its weakest link?* The same can be said in business—a salesperson is only as consistent, effective and successful as they are clear, disciplined and living in integrity with themselves. This integrity means getting *honest* with ourselves about the issues we have that might be setting us back in business—and in life.

While it's an effective professional strategy to separate work and life, they are directly related when it comes to mental, emotional and physical wellness. Clients are surprised by how much of my courses are exercises they'd find in a personal development book or with a mental health specialist. We'll be halfway through the coursework when they recognize that what they *thought* was an issue in their sales funnel or skill set was actually a mental or emotional block due to issues from childhood. They'll sign up with the intention to learn strategy or something about building clientele and walk away in tears realizing what they truly *need* is to love themselves and to grieve. Whether we're saying goodbye to someone who has passed away, a romantic partner from a failed relationship, a person who is no longer our friend, or even a version of ourselves that we used to be … we will need to grieve.

I always tell my clients, "You're going to have to go through the process of grieving, but you will make it through because you are stronger than you will likely ever find out."

I figure there's no way around it … we can either repress our pain and destroy everything we're trying to build in the process, or we can learn to *grieve well*, which is a huge responsibility. This is especially important if we've had traumatic childhoods *and* the concept of grief seems foreign to us. We might think things like,

*I don't know why I have these feelings—my childhood wasn't
even that bad!*
I'd rather make the best of it by choosing positivity.
There's no sense crying over things I can't change.
I forgive my parents—there's nothing left to do!

We're so inundated with personal development information
that *some* of these examples even *sound* healthy. But repressing
grief while forcing positivity or a generalized sense of
forgiveness doesn't heal the wound. Grief is a complex
process; unless we yield fully to it—our subconscious will
store unprocessed trauma until we've recreated the same
situation so many times it feels like a scene from *Groundhog
Day*. It's not enough that we want to move on from the past,
to prevent repeating it: The process of grief is necessary—
especially if thinking about the past feels *numb, blank,* or
difficult to tap into. If the past feels shadowy, or if there is
a lack of clarity, we must examine all of it—reconcile all of
it and get honest—radically honest—with ourselves about
what's not working.

Often, clients will stand on the precipice of healing and
be so horrified at how much work they think it's going to
take—that they hide their faces from it. I know that's what I
did for the better part of 40 years.

They don't understand that not *all* healing is arduous,
painful, or long-suffering. Some of it is downright delightful.
As we access our truth, we build rapport with ourselves. We

become our own advocates—our own teacher, healer and friend.

Over time, we stop being afraid of what we're going to find *under there*, because we learn even our most shadowy parts and consistent pains can be contended with, processed and managed. In turn, *we start to feel better!*

So, I ask my clients to get *real* with themselves about their pasts—which can be challenging ... because children of abandonment and neglect make *a lot* of excuses for the users and abusers in their lives. When we were children, survival was contingent on the stories we told ourselves about *why* we weren't getting what we needed. By shrinking our own observations, opinions, needs and desires—we changed the narratives so we would not have to not face the pain of reality. But at some point, we *must* see the truth.

It is of utmost importance, while considering this concept, that we remember *our* most favorite phrase ...

I am not a victim.

I can imagine what you're thinking: *But Wally—there's no way I can both be honest with myself about what happened and also not feel like a*
slighted,
sad,
deprived,
abused,
angry
victim.

And you know what? That's valid. You'd be surprised to know that *feeling* those uncomfortable, unprocessed feelings is the fastest ticket to *reasoning* yourself out of victimhood. Both realities exist inside this kernel of truth. You were a victim of terrible circumstances. The repercussions of someone else's actions caused you to feel immeasurable pain. To survive, you numbed out that pain with any medication you could find: Drugs, alcohol, sex, food, cigarettes, work, etc .... and even just avoided it altogether.

Overcoming that pain means awakening to that pain and reconciling it once and for all—so you can be triumphant. It is this process of radical responsibility that makes us the heroes of our own stories. I tell my clients to consider pain as a tunnel—it's something we walk through; it's not a stopping place ... *we get through it* ... and on the other side is a more sober understanding of who we are.

Sober being the keyword. So, I have to ask—

What happened to you?

Do you even know? Can you even remember?

Part of coming into integrity with ourselves is validating our emotions and experiences and that all starts with awareness of what the problem is and where it first started. Then, we must transcend past that point, which looks like reading the past with as much objectivity as possible. Grieving through what happened is only one consideration. The second consideration is—

What did you make that mean about you?

One of the hardest truths I've had to process is that my dad's actions toward me that *felt* personal were *not* personal. His issues were about him. But I had to allow Little Wally to have his perception, validate his pain around that perception and then bring him into adulthood with a new toolbox for how to perceive pain. My dad and mom did the best that they could and I now understand that.

The scariest part about truth is that—while I very much believe there is a divine absolute Truth—most *truths* are a matter of perception. Isn't it terrifying to consider that we are active participants in the way we perceive and retell what happened to us?

Believe it or not, there is a whole modality of therapy *dedicated* to the power of storytelling. In the 1980s, David Epston and Michael White made waves in the behavioral science world with *narrative therapy*. Stephen Madigan details their research in *Narrative Therapy: Theories of Psychotherapy*. He covers important aspects of the practice, including the value of asking ourselves *good, thoughtful, meaningful* questions, sifting through *all* future possibilities (when working through anxiety) to position ourselves for the highest good and challenging the meaning we've ascribed to other people's actions—the latter of which is a major key to defining our truths.[12]

---

12 Stephen Madigan, *Narrative Therapy* (Washington, DC: American Psychological Association, 2019).

Don Miguel Ruiz, author of *The Four Agreements: A Practical Guide to Personal Freedom*, takes not personalizing one's pain one step further:

When we really see other people as they are without taking it personally, we can never be hurt by what they say or do. Even if others lie to you, it is okay. They are lying to you because they are afraid. They are afraid you will discover that they are not perfect. It is painful to take that social mask off. If others say one thing, but do another, you are lying to yourself if you don't listen to their actions. But if you are truthful with yourself, you will save yourself a lot of emotional pain. Telling yourself the truth about it may hurt, but you don't need to be attached to the pain. Healing is on the way and it's just a matter of time before things will be better for you.[13]

Ruiz's complex way of considering truth helps us *accept* the imperfection of our circumstances—while simultaneously embracing *and* detaching from the pain of what happened. It's saying,

My dad harmed me; while there is no excuse for his unacceptable behavior, I see that it was a byproduct of his pain and deficit—therefore, it was not about me. Because it

---

13 Ruiz, Don Miguel, and Janet Mills. *The Four Agreements,* 1997.

was not a reflection of my worth, I can separate myself from it. I can see his humanity. I can forgive him—not because he asked for it, not because he deserves it ... but because I deserve to be spiritually, mentally and emotionally free.[14]

And that's why it's important ... to understand what happened to you; that's why I share with you what happened to me. As the valiant, tragic heroes of our own lives—we are given the opportunity to wield the sword of truth. As we ration out what is real and what is fragmented—we embrace the art of being *measured and* we come into a place of integrity with ourselves that enables us to feel fully, grieve well and heal completely.

The Five Stages of Grief

Grief is the private agreement we make with ourselves to let go of the idea we once had about how things *should* have gone. I *should* have had a dad who loved and respected himself. It hurts me *for* him; it hurts me for everyone affected by him that this was not the case. I wish it could have been different—but it wouldn't be my story if everything had gone the way I thought it *should have.*

My mom should have never been a smoker. It's dramatic irony—if you think about it. Here, the audience has this

---

14 Ruiz, Don Miguel, and Janet Mills. *The Four Agreements,* 1997.

character who is so anxious about everything from survival, to finances, to physical health—that she turns to smoking to cope—a detriment to all three things. And we can do nothing but grieve because it's senselessly tragic. It's not what *should* have happened. But it is what happened, nevertheless.

This is the unpredictable part of suffering—and it happens to all of us. We fall madly in love—certain that our partner will never leave; we vow *for better or for worse*, but when the worst of the worst comes, we can't sustain the promises we made. And we lose. We put ourselves through college to prepare ourselves to land the job and we might even make it to the final round of the interview to learn—we were rejected from the only dream we ever had.

Could it be? It can't be. It wasn't supposed to be this way.

It was supposed to be ... *good.*

When bad times come and there is a radical deviation from the way we think something should have gone, we must first grieve the dream of what it could have been. Sometimes this helps us so clearly see the raw deal we were served that it resolves a lot of conflict about the rest of what happened. We might come to find that what we think we are in pain about is not actually what happened—but what *never* happened. After the illusion is diffused by rationality, the reality of what took place might become more palatable (in some cases).

In other cases, grief is compounded. Especially in survivors with C-PTSD (*complex* post-traumatic stress disorder)—a diagnosis that implies inordinately stressful circumstances took place over a sustained period of time.

In 1969, Elizabeth Kübler-Ross established her theory on the five stages of grief:

The five stages—denial, anger, bargaining, depression and acceptance—are a part of the framework that makes up our learning to live with the one(s) we lost. They are tools to help us frame and identify what we may be feeling. But they are not stops on some linear timeline in grief.[15]

In my experience, grief is never linear. Sometimes we go from denial to depression and then back to denial. Other times, we experience more than one of the stages at the same time. There's no cut-and-dried approach to grieving and certainly, there is no set timeline. More often than not, it lies dormant until a trigger happens: The trace scent of my dad's aftershave in the grocery store, the smell of Newport cigarettes, the taste of marinara sauce, the sound of an old cartoon jingle, or the sensation of hunger in my stomach. Then, my body remembers what my mind has shelved away ... and I have to take some time to sit with my pain. I'm not always great at it—but if the pain calls, I must go. That's the rule to getting better and even though it's not always linear

---

15 "Quotes." EKR Foundation, 12 Sept. 2019, https://www.ekrfoundation.org/elisabeth-kubler-ross/quotes/.

... there truly are five defined stages—and likely many more, especially if we consider the baseline anxiety and depression that tends to come with the territory of growing up in a turbulent home.

Wally Bressler's Five Stages of Grief

1. Denial: *Eating Pizza*

As a kid, *denial* tasted like a large cheese pizza from Bob's in Nashua. There were times that Dad would sneak out at dinner time and bring home a pizza from Bob's, which today is still my favorite pizza on the planet. It was a fairly cheap and tasty way to keep us all fed. We were an *around the table* family, even though I can't remember our conversations consisting of anything other than tense, drawn-out pauses or being told that I needed to slow down because I was eating too fast. Mom and Dad would often ask direct questions about how school was going (that neither I nor my siblings wanted to answer). Mom would nod kindly and eat her food while the rest of us would tread lightly in case something would come up to upset Dad. Oftentimes, we'd dig in, not realizing the spaces of ourselves that were deadening as the years passed. We accepted—*this is just how family is.* This was especially true for me before high school because I was getting in trouble so often in school. Sure, Dad was a hardass—but he wasn't an *abuser*, especially not in the '70s. *Right?*

One of the more interesting elements of my work is that I coach clients from every generation. The standards for what is considered acceptable and healthful parenting have significantly changed over the decades. As we've made major strides in understanding childhood development, the vast majority of millennials have abandoned the discipline tactics of their parents. We've healthfully transitioned from belts and wooden spoons in the '70s and '80s to being *grounded* and made to do consequential manual labor in the '90s and early 2000s and finally to emotional regulation tents—and actually teaching our kids how to process anger, take a break, breathe through their pain and communicate. Because we've made so many strides, our parents' poor discipline strategies are usually seen as entirely egregious or *a sign of the times* ... with little in between. It's very important for my clients to wrap their minds around the fact that—*it was both*.

The brains of adult children of neglect and abuse have a profoundly difficult time identifying mistreatment early on in their healing. This is why it's common for generational *burdens* to repeat themselves—for children of abuse to end up in abusive dynamics later in life. They've seen the world through tinted lenses since they were born—it's the only perspective they have. Because of this ... they often don't realize the complex trauma living in their bodies until they are much older in life. They wake up wondering why their life is in shambles ... not realizing they've acted out every pattern of the generation before them. This obliviousness to chronic pain (mental, emotional and physiological) is a huge part of *denial*.

We see this phase portrayed in TV shows and movies— often one-dimensionally. Sure—sometimes it really is as simple as that. It can sound like,

No, my wife isn't leaving me—I don't accept that.

My business is doing just fine! We just had a slow quarter.

Having a few beers each night doesn't constitute addiction.

Just because my dad hit me sometimes—doesn't make him an abuser.

But more often, I've found denial is so ambient it's woven into our day-to-day patterns in ways that are hidden, even to ourselves. It's believing a Snoopy toothbrush is a big enough gift to be symbolic of unconditional love and redeem the whole. It's the smiling and nodding at the dinner table, the way our parents did—when we are being harmed by a partner who *loves us*. It's the buy-in ... given by the submissive party in the power dynamic of any toxic relationship. Whether it's familial, friendship, or business relationships—*denial* is made up of the covert contracts we make with our aggressors to play a complicit role. To keep surviving. Because *it didn't happen*—right? And even if it happened ... *it surely wasn't as bad as I remember it*.

2. Anger: *Acting Out in School*

When I sat inside, hearing the other children playing in the yard at my ninth birthday party—I experienced a myriad of emotions that were more than my childhood mind could articulate. But the pattern I observed consistently with my dad was that his punishments never matched the crime; moreover—they involved neglect and deprivation of resources and often accompanied by the silent treatment. Though I had no discipline structure to compare it to, I sensed I was being fundamentally wronged by the two people in my life who were supposed to protect me. My dad was the aggressor; his behavior communicated messages like, *I am committed to misunderstanding you; it doesn't matter what you say, it doesn't matter what you do—I am right, you are wrong; there's no way out of this.*

Being put in a position of helplessness and/or voicelessness at any age incites primal anger. I wasn't allowed to vocalize my thoughts or feelings and if I confided in my mom, she'd rationalize my anger and tell me to *be the peacemaker.* Never acknowledging that she and Dad were the true *crazymakers* in the dynamic. Namely due in part to her own grief, her own denial that was so intricately woven together with her own repressed rage. Chicken Little was a neurotic mess, because if she was worried ... she had no room to feel angry. Angry about how my dad treated her. Angry about how my dad treated us ... and angry at herself for a lifetime of internal betrayal.

My similar relationship to anger began at a young age, but unlike my mom—*I was all boy.* I acted out in class, knocked the crap out of some kids who truthfully *started it* and found myself holed up in the principal's office more times than I could count. I was fuming and I had nowhere to put it—save the futile attempts my parents made to put me in athletic activities. Because I lived in a home where control was used in addition to discipline, I wasn't allowed the autonomy of communicating how I felt. Even if I'd wanted to, I wouldn't have had the language to put to the feeling. Even if I'd had the language—Dad wouldn't have cared. And it was that reality that kept my fist and jaw clenched throughout my entire childhood. I was angry because I had to advocate for myself *against* my guardian. It was too much to process as a child and even now I sometimes have trouble navigating the anger as an adult. But—as my own caretaker, I have equipped myself with the tools I need to *feel* my anger and understand what it was trying to tell me. Although I couldn't create boundaries in relation to my dad, I could retrospectively create the internal boundaries that would protect Little Wally's demeanor from being broken every time his dad reacted disproportionately to circumstance. In turn, I've become my own guardian—committed to protecting, hearing and empowering myself ... no matter the cost.

3. Bargaining: *Putting on the Mask*

For a salesperson, negotiation comes with the territory. I've spent decades showing people how to improve their lives with products and programs that I believe in (and admittedly some I didn't believe as much in, earlier in my career). While strong negotiation skills can *only* be cultivated through things like an adept understanding of the business, self-confidence and great communication—the *bargaining* skills I learned through becoming a fantastic liar (throughout my childhood and my marriage) serve as an example of how we can make learned behavior work for us. Because my family was always walking on eggshells, people-pleasing was the specific way I bargained for things like nourishment, affirmation, attention, praise and care. This included trying to win friends over in school by giving them my Christmas and birthday gifts—because I was desperate to be liked, even if I had very little. The covert, relational contracts I made with my parents, friends and educators transitioned into adulthood with my partners, colleagues and children. Though the power dynamics and relationships changed, the tactic never did.

If I give you my toys—you have to stay.
I will make you laugh if you promise not to beat me up.
I will tell you the truth—as long as you don't punish me.
If you're going to punish me whether I'm good or bad—I will commit a crime that fits the punishment.
If I can't get your attention through positive behavior, I'll get it through acting out.
God, I promise if you just save my marriage, I'll never cheat again.

If I get out of this bad business deal—I'll be honest.
If I can cover my tracks from the feds—I'll stop making bad decisions with money.
If you just help me out with this one, I'll show you've I've changed.

While my bargaining started with my young grief and was originally melancholic—it took on a more sinister form when compounded by the ramifications of trauma. Because I was raised to cater, to pander, to please—I strived for every ounce of love I ever received. The bar for my parents' approval was always so high that my internal motivator shifted from,

How can I get my way in this scenario?
To
What can I get away with?
And I promise you—I tried to get away with a lot.
People don't realize that bargaining is not always a plea deal—sometimes it can take the shape of low-balling. For me, it looked like a combination of both. As I stood in front of a judge, settling for a plea deal, I promised myself and God that I would make my life better *if I could just get out of going to prison.*
The cool thing about God is that He knew to break the generational cycle I was living in—the most merciful thing to do was to let me hit rock bottom. He allowed my lies to catch up with me and I was able to feel the pain of the bottom line.

I had no bargaining power at that point. I had lost. The only way to the other side of the horrible existence I had created for myself was going through that process. And it was this profound loss that enabled me to *finally* begin keeping my own promises.

4. Depression: *Watching Pornography*

Pornography is an obvious, unfortunate reality in the lives of most teenage boys. But it entered my life—tragically—as a byproduct of sexual abuse, at an incredibly young age. I was barely 11 before it'd claimed most of my spare time. And the consistent release of *feel-good* chemicals to my brain gave me a boost from my perpetual sadness as a kid, fueled largely by abuse and isolation. When I was sent to my room without food, it left me to consume other things ... things that provided an immediate hit that would sustain me for several hours at a time. But I'd inevitably crash in between—and return to it. Until my internal world was a roller coaster of pain, shame and prolonged stints of numbness in between.

This coping cycle stayed with me through adulthood and after I was left to fully feel and face the consequences of my own actions—the sadness of my childhood unexpectedly caught up to me. In October of 2019, I was so overcome with depression that I considered taking my own life. It was one of my heaviest experiences and it ultimately served as a rebirth. At my darkest hour, there was a final spark that ignited my will to live. It was the catalyst to my reaching out to get the adequate help I needed.

Through the help of an insightful therapist, I was able to start addressing the depression itself—and the complex emotions that fueled it, including inward-facing anger, humiliation, sadness, hopelessness, shame and loneliness. Once I could name these emotions and begin to regulate them—I could begin to reconcile the past at a pace that was reasonable for my healing journey.

5. Acceptance: *Starting Over*

Hitting the reset button on my life after beginning therapy was *not* easy. I had decades of grief to process, in addition to learning how to be compassionate toward myself for my mistakes. By my 50s, I had transitioned from victim to villain. I'd destroyed my marriage, been a subpar parent and spent my time in the clink.

My newfound appreciation for life was enough to keep me afloat, but that's not to say my negative thought life and difficult feelings went away instantaneously. The key difference between my life before rock bottom and the *acceptance* phase of my grief journey was that I was living a life fueled by gratitude as opposed to the victim mentality.

When I was released from prison, there was no returning to my previous life. I had no job, no money and an abysmal reputation. I was at the complete mercy of other people—to house me, to employ me, to feed me, until I got back on my feet. In the evening, the bed felt softer; meals were more savory and I enjoyed them more—with true thankfulness; every dime in my bank account was fulfilling in its own measure—it was no longer about obtaining more; I had recompensed past the point of *lying* to people. Dishonesty was no longer worth the fallout. I wanted to tell the truth.

The *acceptance* phase of my grieving process was where I decided I wanted to take radical responsibility for my own future. It didn't mean feeling great about the things that my parents did. It didn't mean shelving those painful emotions in an effort to *stay positive*. It was me saying, *I don't have the stamina to continue these terrible habits and generational traumas, so I'm going to rewire my brain.*

It still takes hard work, commitment and effort; I am *still* in the process of healing. And as previously mentioned, what I accept in the morning is still something I might experience anger or sadness about by evening. Progress is taking these difficult emotions in stride and understanding they are just temporary. I don't have to return to old vices, because I have a proper tool kit and support system in place to help me navigate difficult emotions and choose to respond instead of reacting.

Making Meaning

Later in her career, Elizabeth Kubler-Ross began collaborating with grief expert David Kessler, who made an addition to the initial *five stages of grief*. He proposed that there was, in fact, a sixth stage that utilized the art of storytelling to *make meaning* of the pain we've experienced. In his book *Finding Meaning: The Sixth Stage of Grief*, Kessler writes,

> *Meaning is relative and personal. Meaning takes time. You may not find it until months or even years after loss. Meaning doesn't require understanding. It's not necessary to understand why someone died in order to find meaning. Even when you do find meaning, you won't feel it was worth the cost of what you lost. Your loss is not a test, a lesson, something to handle, a gift, or a blessing. Loss is simply what happens to you in life. Meaning is what you make happen. Only you can find your own meaning. Meaningful connections will heal painful memories.*[16]

I tell my clients *meaning is what you make it*—and I emphasize the power of our intentions. As we reclaim our narratives, we get to determine who we become by examining how we were shaped. We take action, knowing nothing is definitive unless we decide it is. The meaning I've made in my life is most evident in my work with clients. Every day, I use the triumphs of my story to inspire bravery in the lives of others as they thoughtfully infuse meaning into their own.

---

16 Kessler, David. *Finding Meaning*. Scribner, 2019.

The Physiology of Grief

I've always been a bit of a visual learner. So, there was nothing more impactful to me than the metaphor of having to be alone with my thoughts in my 48-plus square foot cinder block prison cell. The confinement had always been there—from the early years when Mom or Dad would lock me away in my room. One painful isolation yielded another and I found Big Wally had just as much difficulty managing foreign emotions as Little Wally.

So, I took to the exercise facilities to begin working on my physical fitness. This was even before I learned the benefits of altering our physiology in therapy. Not only did I find this helped me stay distracted from the prison blues—it mitigated the anger that would intermittently surface as a byproduct of my circumstances and surroundings. I didn't know at the time that movement would play a significant role in my processing the complex trauma that was stored in my physical body. Over time, I would come into a better understanding of the five stages of grief and how they still present somatically.

Whether it's in feelings of exhaustion—due to denial; tension in my head, jaw and neck–due to anger; a lump in my throat, or pervasive heaviness and soreness in my eyes– due to enduring sadness … I now can better identify difficult feelings through paying attention to bodily sensations—in turn, I can care for myself more intentionally.

When we are faced with the complex pain that has been stored in our physical body for decades–it can send our brains into complete overload. Emotional pain can be managed when we do yoga, go for a walk, or try a new cycling class.

It doesn't have to be strenuous—in fact, it's better if it's in service to your mental health as opposed to with some grandiose weight-loss goal in mind. Listening to our physical bodies and the type of exercise it wants—in relation to the emotions we're feeling only increases our emotional intelligence as we build trust between our physical body and minds through recovery.

***

So, I'm sure you're wondering—*OK, Wally, but where is the stopping point? When does this terrible grief end?* The profound answer is—*never*. We are all in a process of some sort of grief, *more frequently than we realize.* To quote Seneca—

Every new beginning comes from some other beginning's end.[17]

Every season comes to a close—the wonderful ones and the terrible ones. We land a new job; we get laid off. We have an incredibly tight month; we land a new client. One relationship ends; we meet someone new. We see death. We see birth. We see every obstacle in between. The only thing guaranteed is that this cycle will continue, so we might as well learn to grieve with a sense of pride and reverence for life—*celebration, even.*

---

17 Seneca, "Quote," n.d.

The hero's journey is one of many challenges and triumphs. It wouldn't make for a great story if he made it through life unscathed. He has tales of war, battle wounds and a lifetime of revelations before his chapters come to a close. Without the hero's grief process—there would never be growth. Without his suffering—he would never experience appreciation. That was true for the *tragically heroic* Walter Bressler.

Had Big Wally never made every abhorrent bad choice and mistake of his adulthood, he would have never done the work of becoming the sober, dependable, *safe* victor—who faced his demons in a valiant effort to save Little Wally.

And so, it is with patience, endurance, a commitment to self-examination and a profound sense of gratitude for my life and my recovery, that I pick up my sword—*and I grieve.*

4

TRUTH OR CONSEQUENCE

By the time I started playing little league at age 10, I was a masterful liar. The end of my first season marked one of the most memorable times that I got caught—an experience that became a microcosm of my upbringing: a cycle of never-ending dishonesty, hiding and punishment. This was a shame because I enjoyed the sport itself—playing ball on the freshly cut grass, watching the game from behind the fence of the dugout, and being the member of a team. What I didn't enjoy was scanning the bleachers every game to find my parents *weren't there*. While their reasons were valid, I began to build resentment about them being tied up at work or trapped in traffic on the commute home.

They were always unavailable. So, instead of begging them for rides to and from practice, I carpooled to practices and games with my teammates, where I'd absorb the praises of the other kid's parents, who *somehow* found a way to be there. Call it retaliation, but I'd spent the entire season benefiting from my parents' absence—I got a thrill out of lying to them about how many hits I'd gotten throughout the season; my mother's face would light up as I fabricated details about each game.

"Wally ... how is little league going?" she'd ask while rotating helpings around the dinner table.

And that was my spotlight moment, my evening cue *to entertain* the family with my cooked-up stories and fantastical half-truths. To a perfect stranger, I probably sounded like a mini–Babe Ruth ... impressive with all my raw talent, exceptional hand–eye coordination and ardent love of the game. But my animated storytelling abilities exceeded any gift I had on the field. In reality, I was the chubby kid who had made no hits all season and could hardly break into a full run between bases before the ball soared over my head and into the mitt of the nearest baseman.

"You're out!" the umpire would yell—usually an athletic kid with clout among the rest and a *roaring-fans section* full of parents, aunts, uncles and possibly even a babysitter.

The second to last game of the season was no different, except for the shared disappointment of our entire team when our coach sent a pitcher to the mound, out of rotation, because he had just pitched a game the day before. In turn, we were forced to forfeit.

Paying no regard to the listening ears around me, I walked into the infield and yelled, "This sucks!" at the top of my lungs (because it did).

Within seconds, I felt the intense sting of my father's death grip on my ear. To my surprise, my father made it to that game just in time to catch the last inning and witness my outburst. I didn't realize he was there as I stopped looking for my parents to show up at games.

Suffice it to say ... our interaction on the field didn't go well.

"Walter Bressler. You will never act like this in front of other people!" he commanded loudly enough to get the attention of my teammates, who seemed to be as wide-eyed and afraid of his booming voice as I was.

"No more baseball!" he yelled as I followed him to the parking lot in a stupor.

The season's worth of lying about my exploits on the field caught up to me the very next week ... the final week of the season. Somehow, I was able to finagle my way into going to the game despite my father's proclamation that I was forever "done with baseball" the week before.

At the end of the game, Joey Palermo hopped into the back seat of our car after my mother had agreed to give him a ride home. As we rode together, she asked if I'd gotten a hit during the game. I said "No", not wanting to lie in front of Joey. She looked at me in the rearview mirror and said, "That's OK, you got lots of hits this season."

Without skipping a beat, Joey shouted and laughed condescendingly. "No, Mrs. Bressler! Wally hasn't had a *single* hit all season!"

My mother glanced at me again in the rearview mirror, but this time her expression was one of anger and disappointment, a look only a mother could give to her unruly child. And in her silence, she communicated everything: I was in *big* trouble ... I was *caught*.

Naturally, I began to feel claustrophobic in the back seat of the car. There was no room to escape or breathe and I just sat there—embarrassed, hot and red-faced, looking straight ahead the rest of the way home. When we finally arrived, my worst fear of feeling my father's rage came to pass and I was as disproportionately punished as I'd always been.

While the consequences of my behavior were intended to keep me from telling lies, they usually did the opposite. They incited so much shame and guilt inside me that a subsequent cycle of more polished, articulate lies was kicked off. I became practiced with the things I said, not out of malice initially—usually just as a means of survival—but never entirely separated from the anger I felt toward my parents. I was 11 years old when the thrill of lying began to entice me. I started getting off on being dishonest with my parents, addicted to the high of omission and embellishment. My stories were the one place I was completely in control and my being the narrator meant I could make myself out to be the hero ... even if my behavior was antagonistic to everyone involved.

By 16, I was skilled at getting what I wanted from the world by deceiving others. Because I was also a sex addict, I learned to manipulate girls for attention and physical affection.

I'd schmooze them to get them to go on dates with me while lying to my parents about my whereabouts. Our dates would include me buying beer for everyone using my fake ID, going to dance clubs until they closed—or we sobered up—and ending the evening having unprotected sex in the back of my parents' car or at one of the local ball fields … whichever worked for them (how romantic).

Afterward, I'd drive home, still drunk sometimes, and sneak in after curfew. I'd relish the fact that I *never* got caught. And the more I did it, the more believable my lies became, even in my sloppier moments. One of my more reckless memories was the time I drove to the store for my parents in my mother's car. While trying to *be cool*, I accidentally drove over a median and scraped the bottom of the car so badly that the oil pan never worked correctly again. When I got home, I made up some fantastic story about how I'd seen an animal and swerved. For whatever reason, they believed me.

It's important to note that my dishonesty was rooted not only in my ardent hope to not be punished, but also in my desire for my parents' approval, but it quickly devolved into a self-deception so dense I could no longer find myself in the midst of it. I forfeited my internal compass at a young age, so finding *true north* was almost impossible when it came to major life decisions.

Luckily for me, my mother was an educator. So, in the aimlessness of my junior and senior years, she made it her goal to *make sure* I was going to college. It also helped that she and my father had let me join the football team and that I was actually a decent player.

And to my benefit, being on the team meant being moderately popular; therefore, it incentivized me to keep my grades high. I lettered during my junior and senior years and later went on to play ball at Hamilton College, where I was a four-year letter-winner. In high school, good grades and football were the bright spots of my academic career and the things my parents could be proud of. These things distracted them, so I hid from them the rest of the choices I was making.

Influenced largely by my mother, I declared English as my major during my freshman year. It seemed like the easiest choice; plus, I had my mind on other things. My introduction to college inflated my love of partying and socializing. In between drinking with the guys on the football team and the fraternity I was rushing, I was committed to sustaining my years of addiction to food, porn and television. I also started struggling with severe anxiety and debilitating depression.

By May of my freshman year, I wanted to leave. But I knew my mother would have killed me; after all, my parents had saved every penny they had to help fund my education. Fortunately, a meaningful conversation with my position coach, Paul Adey, gave me the boost I needed to stay. Plus, I knew I couldn't let it go to waste. Fueled by negative motivation all four years, I limped through college and faced the penultimate panic of finishing out my senior year without the prospect of a job. It was so bad that I woke up at 4:30 a.m. on Sunday, the week before graduation, anxious and panicked that I had nothing to go to after college was over.

I wasn't alone in this issue. The year was 1991 and I had been out of college for around 12 months, filling in as a substitute teacher at my old high school while living at home. Due to the slowly recovering economy, many people were having issues finding employment. America was gradually extracting itself from the first Gulf War; there were still negative effects of a double-dip recession; inflation was twice what it would be the next year; and the stock market was just starting to chug along again.

I would wake up in the morning and come to the kitchen table for breakfast only to see the employment section of the paper folded in my seat, with every job circled that my mother thought I should apply for *immediately*.

Having very few life skills, destabilizing mental health issues (that only I knew about) and a practically irrelevant major, I knew I was in trouble. I wanted both to survive and to please my parents ... so I exhausted my options.

And finally, I got a customer service job at Putnam

Investments in Boston, Massachusetts. On the side, I did what I knew best: I used my gregarious personality and large frame to make supplemental income as a bartender and doorman. After a few years at Putnam, I made my way to the sales desk, which was one of the very few good decisions I'd made in my tumultuous first quarter century on Earth..

I hadn't realized it at the time and was in no position to steward it, but I was one of the *lucky* ones who had found my calling at a very young age, something that never deterred me from fallout but still preserved my hope in the midst of it. Like many of the clients I work with, I wasn't initially comfortable on the phone. The voices of reason that would shape my later career inspired my earliest days of sales. I devoured a steady diet of content from personal development authors including Brian Tracy, Zig Ziglar and Tony Robbins.

When I had trouble *being Wally*, I would just pretend to be them on the phone. I *faked it* until the sale was made. Though my older self would lend 20-something Wally different advice, this means-to-an-end approach *did* get me more sales, which meant more bonuses. And more ... *money.*

Earning money lit my serotonin-craving brain up like nothing I'd ever felt. It was my *shiny new vice,* dangerously tied to survival and social status in a way the others weren't. The most dangerous thing about money is that—in and of itself—it is not a bad thing. But because I'd never had a fighting chance of living in integrity with myself (or understanding what that meant), I didn't *know* I was predisposed to becoming obsessed with having and making money. I was doomed from the start. All I needed was a catalyst for decline and when Dad ended up in the emergency room with heart complications later that year ... I had one.

Around my dad's 49th birthday, he began showing symptoms that my mother and the family physician interpreted as a gallbladder attack. After a trip to the hospital revealed a blocked artery, the doctors tried unsuccessfully to put in a stent. In turn, they decided to do an emergency bypass, which prompted a midnight trip to the hospital for my mom and me.

Before my father's surgery began, we were able to visit his room; despite the evident fear on his face, the first words he said to my mother were, "Your make-up looks gorgeous." It was so unlike him to say such a thing that I suspected we were in trouble. Still, the doctor said there was a 92 percent chance that everything would be *great*. Once he was in surgery, we sat for hours in the waiting room, anxiously awaiting news; I slept while Mom paced the floors. Finally, we were allowed to see him.

After the surgery, he stayed in the hospital for a day or so, then we took him home and made it through Thanksgiving.

The Friday after, I returned to Boston; and when I walked through the door of the office, I called my mother to check in and asked if I could speak to Dad.

"I'm feeling great," he said. "I love you very much. We were lucky to have you here."

For the first time in my life, I felt my father *meant* the words he was saying. When I told him I loved him back, I realized how much I meant to them too. That moment kept us afloat through the night and kept me steady through Saturday, just before my shift at the local pub. That was until I got a frantic call from my mother right before I left for work that hijacked my nervous system.

"Your father's had another heart attack. The ambulance is here. Wally, you need to come home."

I drove through the night from Boston in record time. The darkness around me was a blur. I arrived at the hospital to the sight of my family weeping and holding each other outside the operating room. Finally, the doctor came out and confirmed our greatest fears—he was gone.

The doctor asked if we wanted to see Dad one last time. Through the haze of being in complete shock, we said yes. Together, we entered the operating room to his lifeless body. His face was sullen and his skin was gray. Machines beeped around him; he had a tube in his mouth and blood down the front of his gown. I vacillated between numbness and confusion about my numbness. Though we were all crying, I wasn't exactly sure what my crying meant at the time.

While my mother was doubled over weeping, the most I

could offer was a pat on the back. I stood and watched for what felt like forever. Then I left the hospital and drove back to what had so quickly become *Mom's house*.

We sat around the table that night, noticing how our surroundings hadn't changed, but everything had somehow become foreign. A friend of the family who was a priest came over to comfort us, along with a friend and former coach of mine, Bob DeMello and his wife Kathy. In my head, all that played out was what *should* have been happening, all in such stark contrast to *what was*.

Sentimentally, we all cried and shared memories about my father. While I entertained my family member's stories, I realized I'd had so few good experiences with him that it felt forced to muster emotion over someone else's nostalgia.

By early morning, the glowing, brown winter sky streamed through my window and light snowflakes began to fall. It covered the ground through December 4th, 1991— the day my dad was buried. And of course, the whole thing was a big, Italian, Catholic funeral with lots of *dynamic* family members expressing bold opinions and emotions as they heralded the traditions of the generations before them.

My Uncle Roger and Aunt Pat (my mother's sister and her husband) rented a limo for the family that day; we climbed in wearing our Sunday best and said little on the ride. When we arrived at the church, the limo door was opened by Dad's colleagues. His final position was one he was able to maintain for a handful of years and he seemed to enjoy it. He was a letter carrier who seemed to have built strong relationships with people along his route. Complete strangers wept all around us; fellow carriers queued at the back of the church to honor my dad. *Everyone* seemed to have fond memories of my father. But as I observed the smiling photograph of him next to his casket, I couldn't remember many times when we'd actually *laughed* together. While there might have been one or two, my mind was blank. So I sat there, forcing myself to grieve a stranger who I had known my whole life.

I comforted my mother as best I could through the reception, packed up some food to take home with me, put on comfortable clothes, then drove back to Boston to begin the next chapter of my life, a life no longer encumbered by my *biggest* critic ... or so I thought.

Irrefutable Integrity

Returning to work gave me the chemical high I needed to distract myself from grieving my father. The love of money is a complex addiction because it's more than just craving material gain. It's an addiction—to strife, to leveling up and to distract ourselves with a *hustle* mentality. This presents a problem on several fronts, but ultimately, it keeps us in a constant game of *keep-up*. And for those addicted to money, this desire to reach the top of the top is dangerous because no accomplishment is ever great enough, no amount of money is ever great enough, no promotion is ever outstanding enough and we quickly become bored with the material possessions we were, at one point, dying to afford.

Our lifestyle becomes the most impeccable lie of all; with all its highlights, we deceive ourselves, not to mention that I spent years in marketing and sales, which has a reputation for deception *for a reason*. While it is a gross generalization to say "sales is bad," there would be no need for my niche if it was *easy* to live in integrity with oneself and also work in sales. Unfortunately, I didn't always live a life of integrity when I started my career ... which never stopped catching up with me. This is why I've been so committed to bringing *truth* to my coaching program and clients. While there might be ample roads for redemption (arguably more than we deserve), it's better to lay a foundation of honesty and do things right from the beginning. This is why I am grateful that *Phone Sales Secrets* has given me the platform to promote a lifestyle of *irrefutable integrity*—with oneself and with others.

Having *irrefutable integrity* means that my clients and I are committed to operating with the most honesty we can muster in every area of our lives. It means we get clear with ourselves about our growth points; we take *radical responsibility* for our lives and tell the truth with as much strength, consistency and authenticity as we can muster.

When we experience the temptation to self-deceive creeping in, we explore the shame, fear and resistance at the core of that desire. In turn, we become salespeople the public can trust ... because we trust ourselves.

In *The Four Agreements*, Don Miguel Ruiz writes, "Be impeccable with your word. Speak with integrity. Only say what you mean. Avoid using the word to speak against yourself or to gossip about others. Use the power of your word in the direction of truth and love."[18]

When I consider the seamless lying I used to get myself ahead throughout most of my life, I cannot help but think, *"Those were impeccable deceptions."* I carefully considered every possible obstruction to getting what I wanted and navigated around it by manipulating others ... with my words. It was an art, really. Later in my life, I would learn to repurpose this skill to get specific about the truth, communicate my intentions up front and be specific when I screwed up so that I could start to regain the trust of those around me.

Social perception is a huge part of having *irrefutable integrity.* My goal was to wipe the slate so clean that if anyone I knew ever publicly questioned me, there would be a band of people who could serve as witnesses to my outstanding character.

Moreover ... I wanted to be able to privately celebrate how irrefutably *honest* I'd become, as opposed to experiencing the highs and lows of constantly trying to get away with something. While developing *irrefutable integrity,* many of my clients express that they've found a reprieve from the physical symptoms of lying. Brad Branton touches on the

---

18 Ruiz, Don Miguel, and Janet Mills. *The Four Agreements,* 1997.

duress caused by deception in his book *Radical Honesty*. He states, "We all lie like hell. It wears us out. It is the major source of all human stress. Lying kills people."[19]

And he would be right. Think about the adrenaline peaks and crashes the body experiences when trying to keep up with the aftermath of a lie—the black-and-white thinking, the catastrophizing, the interrupted sleep, the turning to vices and the self-deception that erodes our ability to attune to our purpose, drive and goals.

In a study done by Leanne ten Brinke, Jooa Julia Lee and Dana R. Carney, these Berkeley and Harvard researchers studied the physiological effects of dishonesty. They found that it increased cortisol levels, which leads to a myriad of heart health issues, not to mention the fact that lying erodes interpersonal relationships—in romantic, familial and platonic situations. And without these support systems ... we suffer; the compromised relationships of my young life were due largely to dishonesty and secret-keeping and that is where my vices were born.[20]

Later in Brinke, Lee and Carney's studies, they write how witnessing and keeping secrets have parallel effects on our health, which ultimately means the lies we covertly

19 Blanton, Brad. *Radical Honesty*. Dell, 1996
20 Leanne ten Brinke, Jooa Julia Lee, and Dana R Carney, "The Physiology of (Dis)Honesty: Does It Impact Health?," *Current Opinion in Psychology* 6 (2015): pp. 177-182, https://doi.org/10.1016/j.copsyc.2015.08.004.

agree to keep with and for our families have negative long-term consequences on every aspect of our lives.[21] If we were to use that same energy to get adequate help and live in *irrefutable integrity* with ourselves, the past and our families and friends, then our lives and the end of our stories would change.

And *that* is the purpose of *Phone Sales Secrets*.

White Lie Wedding

By 1992, I was thriving in corporate America and unsuccessfully trying to make my mother proud. Both she and my father had always been adamant about my finding work in the corporate world, even though I'd always dreamed of being an entrepreneur and starting my own business. Mom had a way of meddling in my life that was *for my best interest*, but this became her preferred pastime after Dad's death, especially when it came to my personal life. Throughout Mom's career in the education world, she'd met many colleagues who were in the same life stage as her, with sons and daughters in their 20s.

Though I'd gone to school with many of them, Stacie wasn't one of them. When my mom found out from Stacie's

---

21 Leanne ten Brinke, Jooa Julia Lee, and Dana R Carney, "The Physiology of (Dis)Honesty: Does It Impact Health?," *Current Opinion in Psychology* 6 (2015): pp. 177-182, https://doi.org/10.1016/j.copsyc.2015.08.004.

mom that she had just moved out of her house and was having trouble adjusting to living on her own, she had the idea to connect us. So she called me and insisted I take Stacie on a date.

Though I was initially reluctant, I obliged. I went to her apartment with a six-pack of Corona beer and we hung out. To my surprise, we ended up liking each other. We continued talking for a while, but due to personal issues, Stacie couldn't offer consistency in dating. Our connection waned and it didn't pick up again for another four years.

Then, in 1996, Stacie called me. She left a few messages, but I didn't return her phone calls. After she'd exhausted her options, her mother had a *chat* with my mother that resulted in Mom insisting I give Stacie another shot. And when Julia Bressler tells you to do something ... you do it.

So we tried again. We hit it off so well that by 1998, we were married and making plans to build a family. On the outside, we appeared to have a good life, but our relationship was beginning to show compatibility issues we'd intentionally overlooked. We started fighting more than we enjoyed each other; in our 16 years of marriage, having our four children was the only thing that diffused the tension.

Over time, my willingness to work on the marriage waned. Our first eight years together were me giving my best, but soon, my interest in making the relationship work diminished and I started living on autopilot. This left room for the demons of my past—namely lying—to creep back in, which inevitably kept Stacie on edge all the time because she intuitively sensed what was already true. She became all the more controlling and her demands just made me lie more, especially when it came to my career goals.

Like my mother, Stacie was driven by her need for security and the belief that conventional nine-to-five jobs would provide for that need. But I couldn't shake my desire to be an entrepreneur and use my skill set to build a business that I believed in. At the time, I wanted to work for myself and the best way to do that was to get into real estate. I was so adamant about it that I chose to get my real estate license and become an agent without Stacie's agreement.

Despite her efforts, Stacie couldn't bring herself to respect real estate salespeople in general and no amount of my reassurance could make her feel safe about my transitioning to a less conventional career.

This is something I see many of my clients struggle with, namely, non-supportive partners. It's challenging when a person is torn between their partner and the career they love, but I no longer see this as a blatant incompatibility. I tell them what I was unwilling to hear during my marriage: *This is an entirely valid response*, especially when our partners aren't natural risk-takers.

I've observed that it gets better once the money starts coming in. Once my clients' partners realize their income can double or even triple when they start working for themselves, their understanding of entrepreneurship changes. Both parties get a better understanding of what my business associate and friend Cliff Freeman, Jr. calls *the three freedoms*—time freedom, money freedom and location freedom. Cliff is a pioneer in helping real estate agents understand exactly what each of those freedoms means and, more importantly, how to make them a reality in their lives.

Acquiring these freedoms takes time and a significant mental and emotional commitment, but the flexibility they provide undoubtedly brings more job and life satisfaction to people. As a result, their family life reaps the benefits.

That's what the appeal of real estate was to me in the late 1990s and that is what my current coaching business has afforded me—more time and resources to focus on what is important, such as taking trips, showing up to my children's after-school events and being able to work from almost anywhere.

Throughout my curriculum, I can teach people how to cultivate the courage, discipline and perseverance it takes to run an outstanding business. As a result, many of their partners get on board with their vision. When clients address what I refer to as *call reluctance* (which is usually rooted in deeper issues), they begin to see their lives change for the better in every area.

This is largely due to embracing the honesty it takes to work through their personal issues. Eighty percent of new salespeople suffer from call reluctance, as do 40 percent of seasoned salespeople. They get into the business because they think they'll be able to afford a fancy car or a swanky place to live right off the bat, but these things take time.

They have to be willing—willing to try, to fail, to get rejected and to have the humility to get back up and try again. That's where I struggled in the beginning. I hadn't worked through the painful patterns of my upbringing. So when a business deal went bad, I lived with the internalized shame of that and it took a toll on my self-esteem and my marriage.

Because I didn't have the tools to emotionally regulate, it led to a deceptive downward spiral so destructive and concealable that it marked the beginning of the end.

***

Given my addictions, stress level, penchant for lying and ambivalence toward my marriage, it was only a matter of time before I started having sex with women who were not my wife.

To my victim mindset, it made complete sense: I felt that my wife hated me, there was no hope of redeeming our marriage, I couldn't do anything to make her happy, so ... I was going to make myself numb.

I'd started investing as a realtor and when I wasn't out showing houses or looking at deals, I was out cheating on my wife. In the brief times when I was home, I wasn't *seen* by Stacie. She had her own walls up, which presented as being the very devout, extremely overbearing supermom.

I felt like there was always something that came before me. When it wasn't the kids, it was all the work that having kids creates. There was no time for intimacy or connection—or salvaging either of these. She never made time to look me in the face and confirm her greatest fears, namely that I wasn't telling the truth until the day came that she actually caught me cheating on her—a day that marked her life indefinitely. In a sense, we were both living a double life: We'd lied to ourselves first and therein to each other.

While there were parts of us that loved each other, I had never been *in love* with Stacie. This was perhaps the most egregious lie that I'd told her, our families, friends and myself.

The most horrifying part was that I began to notice the worst parts of ourselves manifested in our children in subtle ways. I wish I could say it scared me enough to change. But it wasn't enough for me to address the patterns that had such a strong hold over me and ones that crept up only after I had kids—like yelling.

I yelled at my kids a lot when they were very young; I became my father faster than I could stop it. When I wasn't binge-watching television with them—exacerbating their reliance on media consumption—I was disciplining them harshly, negatively impacting their self-esteem.

While I was escaping my parental duties, I humiliated their mother without her knowledge or ate myself into oblivion and turned to porn for a serotonin boost.

And worst of all—I was *good* at it; I got a high out of living two realities because it made me feel liberated and in control. It required me to be meticulous enough to feel like I was leading an exciting life and as a result, I abandoned morality.

On so many occasions, I could have done the *right thing*. I could have been honest with Stacie, divorced her and become an excellent co-parent to our children. But by that point, I'd self-deceived so much ... I only had space for my enduring selfishness. *I* was all that mattered in my world. And this began to skew my moral compass in ways that I would not be able to come back from.

The Company We Keep

In *Lies We Tell Ourselves: The Psychology of Self-Deception*, Courtney Warren[22] demonstrates how "the areas in which we felt most insecure, unsafe, unloved, uncomfortable, embarrassed, angry and generally unresolved as a child are the areas that we will be most prone to self-deception as an adult."

This was true for me in every relational area of my life. However, like most people and many of the men I was in prison with, I rationalized that the work world was completely exempt from the impact of my choices.

---

22 Frederickson, Jon. *The Lies We Tell Ourselves*, 2017.

That's the most deceptive thing about living in a society where money is a sign of success. It's easy to confuse income and social status with how *well* we're doing, when in reality ... becoming morally bankrupt is one of the easiest ways to make money. It's our responsibility to ensure we're doing business with *irrefutable integrity*—so there's a level of accountability. If we aren't taking a moral inventory of ourselves, the deeply rooted desire to be accepted and survive can upend our lives.

For the kid who always gave his underwhelming Christmas gifts away to be liked, who hoarded food out of fear he would never have enough, whose parents could never afford the latest toys, shoes, or even Cow Tales for lunch ... it was easy to become consumed with the need for approval in the sales world.

Too easily, we end up *selling ourselves*—and *selling ourselves out* in this industry. And we're motivated by money, yes, but also by ego ... to be loved, to be accepted, to be on top. And because so many of us are addicted to gaining each other's affirmation as opposed to honoring our values or tuning in to our gut instinct about the trustworthiness of the people we partner with, we are more likely to tune out the little voice inside ourselves that tells us *something isn't right*. Even worse, we give ourselves reasons to believe that voice is wrong to keep ourselves in the game just a little bit longer.

Warren also states that "The more we lie to ourselves about how we are contributing to our problems, the more harm we will cause to ourselves and our relationships because we will blame others for undesirable aspects of our lives instead of taking responsibility for our role'" That's exactly what I did when I started making bad business deals with the wrong influences in the industry. Some of it was chosen naivety, which a lot of recovery circles will mention is a side effect of childhood trauma. In the short term, it's easier on our conscience to make the obvious truth more palatable, especially when it comes to people we trust doing unethical things. We might see it and want to believe them so badly ... that we deliberately disbelieve anything that factually presents itself against them.

Or we self-deceive by making a one-time exception for them ... over and over and over again. We get creative with excuses for them and sometimes feel liberated in these excuses for ourselves. The bond is sealed with a little bit of collateral. Once both people are doing unethical things, it makes it easier to sign on dotted lines that one or both people don't feel great about.

And that's how fraudulent activity began to happen right in front of my face. Sometimes, I would question what we were doing and my business partner would affirm that *everything was fine.* But it's not something I can play the victim about—or say, "If I had known, I would have done differently."

Because the truth is, I wouldn't have.

If I hadn't learned what red flags look like, allowed myself to be blinded by wealth, turned a blind eye and become complicit in the experience, I would have never hit rock bottom. I would have never learned to distinguish how impacted I am by the negative—and positive—influences of others.

In the ever popular words of Jim Rohn, "You are the average of the five people you spend the most time with ... they determine what conversations dominate your attention."[23]

If these conversations predispose us to self-abandon or self-deceive, we will sabotage excellent opportunities for growth in business, romance, finances and personal development.

It really is about *the company we keep* because it will have a direct impact on who we become. The toughest part of this lesson is that if we are becoming something we can't be proud of, only *we* can be held responsible.

That's why, when we find ourselves in any kind of prison (literal or figurative), we have to accept the fact that it all began with us and the influences we let into our lives.

I recognize, as children of neglect or abandonment, this can be complicated. By the design of nature and nurture, we want to *people-please*. So, *standing up for ourselves* really is as brave as being able to call things out in the moment.

---

23 Jim Rohn, "Quote," n.d.

We need to assertively advocate for our perspective, saying, "Something isn't right. I don't feel good about this. I will not participate in something that doesn't feel true to my standards and values."

It doesn't have to be abrupt or accusatory, but it's best if it's clear and authentic to how we feel. My life would have gone in an entirely different direction if I'd called my "horrible choice" by its actual name: *mail fraud*.

But I didn't.

So when the State of New Hampshire Banking Department began investigating our business in 2006, I sought affirmation regularly from the people with whom I'd created the huge mess, as my stomach was continually in knots knowing ... we were in trouble. Deep trouble—the kind of trouble I could only distract myself from by focusing on *bigger* things.

5

THE BIGGEST LOSER

Can't Win for Losing

I n early 2006, I was almost 140 pounds overweight, miserable and in the throes of emotional eating due to anxiety about the ongoing investigation into my partner's and my fraudulent activity.

Around that time, NBC's *The Biggest Loser* was growing in popularity. One night, while watching it, Stacie—who was pregnant at the time with our fourth child—suggested that I should try out for it. I knew little about reality television, so I shrugged off the idea until the suggestion began circulating in my friend group.

Why not? I thought. What else was I doing besides watching my business associates and friends being questioned day in and day out by the government?

I began by doing research—I bought a few books on how to get on a reality show. Then I called a casting director in

January 2006 who suggested I drive down to Boston for the cattle call (surely they could have thought of a better name, I know).

There, I joined at least one thousand people gathered outside one of Boston's comedy clubs to try out for the show. During the initial casting meeting, enthusiastic contestants would grab a table and sit in groups chatting while the casting directors scanned the crowd for potential.

Some people had to try out—others were selected based on their appearance.

"You have to be good-looking," the casting director said.

This confused me.

"Isn't the point to become good-looking if I get on the show?" I asked.

"We need you to be good-looking now and good-looking later—we want to take you to the next level."

It started to make sense. To be the hero of any story, you've got to have some redeeming qualities. And I figured that, despite my compulsive lying, cheating and dirty business deals, I was at least moderately attractive. I also was entertaining and I figured I could use my sales personality to really captivate the directors at the audition.

A few days later, I sat down with them at a hotel in Boston, answered many of their questions and then made it to the round of putting together a video of who *I am*. Evidently, it went well because I got picked to be on the show. About two months later—yes, it took that long—they called me and told me to pack my bags because I was going to Los Angeles. After making the show, I immediately became concerned because legal issues were starting for me. It took a large dose of humility to call them and explain what was happening—but I was glad to find they said I could still be on the show.

One week later, I was in a California hotel preparing for one full week of intake. The process was extensive—every participant had to have medical exams. They filmed us preparing, eating, talking about our health thus far and working out. On the official opening day of the season, I was a little star-struck when Caroline and Bob came out on the zipline to welcome people to the show.

I was categorized as an at-home contestant. This meant I would be given a strict regimen to follow and have frequent check-ins, with my progress regularly monitored. This also meant if it wasn't my nutritionist calling, it was my doctor or the New Hampshire Banking Department.

The competing stressors started surfacing. As I took away my longest-standing coping mechanism—eating as much as I wanted when I wanted—my anxiety soared.

As such, I had to go on anxiety medication. It didn't help that, at the time, I was having affairs with two different women. Keeping up with the endless lies I was continually weaving was beginning to catch up to me. In turn, I tried to get as tunnel-visioned as possible about my weight-loss goals ... so I could just stop thinking.

Throughout the season, my progress excelled. I ended

up quickly losing 116 pounds while enjoying my time in the spotlight. When it came time for the season finale, the directors wanted all the contestants to fly to Los Angeles for filming.

Naturally, I stopped in Dallas, Texas, for a business trip along the way. There, I snuck in a quick, self-serving rendezvous with one of the women I was having an affair with. Though I was actually in love with the woman I was going to see (and planning to leave Stacie for), our meet-up served as the adrenaline rush I needed to satisfy my addictive mind. In reality, I just wanted to find an escape. But that escape came with a price.

I was completely distracted from my life and dissociated from my body when my business partner decided to stop paying mortgages on people who'd stopped paying their rent. This was completely without my knowledge or consent and without consideration for my well-being and the well-being of my mother and brother, who were also involved with the business.

When I finally found out, I refused to participate. In turn, my partner and I had a disagreement that severed our relationship indefinitely. This scared me, particularly because we were no longer a unified front.

On the one hand, I hoped my breaking ties with someone dishonest would bring me some sort of reprieve. On the other hand, I didn't trust him to play fair with the legal proceedings we'd gotten into. To make matters worse, I had to deliberately compartmentalize my fear because Stacie and I had just had a baby in December of 2006.

By the spring of 2007, I'd put my marriage in serious jeopardy. We were in dire financial straits. In an effort to make things more stable, I took a job in Dallas, Texas. While a move would be more difficult in the short term, I wanted to take care of our family. So we packed up our things and moved to Texas that summer.

Prior to leaving for Texas, Stacie and I began to lose things I'd never bargained for—due to my bad behavior. Our large ticket items were gradually being repossessed, beginning with my car.

It happened under the most embarrassing circumstances possible. My wife was having a candle party with several of her friends. As Stacie innocently relaxed, celebrating the only moment of socializing and peace she'd had in months, I saw the tow truck coming up the street and knew what it meant. They were coming to take away my beloved BMW.

Luckily, the repo man was gracious enough to let me drive my car to the end of the street before he loaded it up on the tow truck. As he drove away, I grieved the vehicle that had sustained my ego for three years, the one I'd purchased to feel important, successful and rich.

I hated that those things couldn't have been farther from the truth. In reality, I was failing my children, Stacie and myself.

Soon after, I ended up having to short-sell our home because we weren't able to pay our mortgage. This was in part because, when we bought the house, I got an adjustable-rate mortgage and the interest rate went from six percent to just under 10 percent. This caused my payments to go to almost $4,000 a month. I kept thinking I'd be able to scale quickly and we would adjust ... but we never did.

Because I didn't have the coping skills to acclimate to external stressors in my life, I began to spin out of control. To make matters worse, my mother had essentially disowned me due to my sinking our mutual business investment.

So when she called me in September of 2007 to tell me that she was dying of lung cancer, I was especially devastated. Not knowing how to approach the issue, I tried to say anything and everything. But my mother had heard it all and she couldn't be sold, negotiated with, or swindled. Our bad real estate deal had destroyed her credit, which she'd worked the last 30 years of her life to preserve. I'd ruined the tail end of her life with my character deficits ... the life of a woman who had never had even a speeding ticket to account for. She remained furious with me as her health declined.

On her deathbed, I pleaded with her to forgive me and she was so upset ... she withheld her forgiveness.

"I'm done," she said.

My mother died being *done* with me.

On the day we buried my mother, I wore a suit my aunt and uncle had to purchase for me because I couldn't afford one on my own.

Throughout her service, I thought about how I'd failed her, my wife and my four children. But the sick sensation of shame only made me feel more panicked and consumptive than ever. Because my marriage had become too fractured for me to confide in my wife, I fought my demons alone in the dark. I didn't have the mental space to carry the grief of everything I'd lost, along with the fear of going to prison for the rest of my life. I wanted clarity. So when the FBI finally called in 2008, I felt equally horrified and relieved to finally have some answers about where my future was headed.

I was fortunate enough to hire one of New Hampshire's best defense attorneys at the time, Mark Howard, who is now a superior court judge in New Hampshire. He let me know that I had options. I could agree to work with the government to get as low a sentence as possible, or I could go to trial.

The trial would cost roughly $75,000 (which would total about $105,000 today) for Mark to defend me.

" ... and if we miss just one signature, or one small sentence, in the one terabyte of data and materials from the case ... we lose. And you're looking at roughly 14 years in prison," Mark said to me.

His words made me the most scared I had ever been in my entire life; remember, I'd lived most of my life up to that point in fear of *something*. I did the math on 14 years in prison and realized that my oldest child, who was 14 at the time, would be roughly 28 when and if I was released in 168 months. In turn, I helplessly softened.

I promised myself, my wife, God and the FBI that I would cooperate as much as possible in hopes of a lighter sentence. To my benefit, they promised me that if I told the truth, I'd get a break; so, I knew I had to watch myself because, let's face it ... I was an incredibly good liar, which was horrible for me in this situation.

Because we were in trouble for suspected mail fraud, I spoke with a couple of assistant U.S. attorneys, FBI agents and two postal inspectors. When the first postal inspector spoke to me, the first thing he said was, "Sorry to hear your mother died."

I thanked him for his sensitivity, knowing that even at its kindest, it was threatening. They were keeping tabs on me—closer than I could have ever imagined.

"Is your brother still living at 707 Rolling Hills Lane?"

"How long ago did your sister move from her previous residence?"

Most of these questions I had trouble answering because I'd been caught up in my personal whirlwind; in my selfishness, I hadn't been paying attention to anyone else's lives for years.

Every question they asked was an underlying threat: They were letting me know that they knew *everything*.

"Don't lie to us. Don't you dare lie to us."

They grilled me for roughly four hours at the initial meeting. After drinking several bottles of water that I pretty immediately sweat through my shirt—with my attorney's assistance and my fear of having five years tacked on to whatever sentence I was going to get for lying — the truth serum paid off.

I worked my potential sentence down from 14 years to five years. It was the first of many grueling investigations that took place over the next five years. In 2011, I finally pleaded guilty to one count of mail fraud. The admission came with a sigh of relief—but it was only momentary because I realized I would have to testify against my former partner.

This meant I had to meet with the FBI regularly.

My initial meeting took place in New Hampshire. The U.S. Attorney's office for the state of New Hampshire flew me out of state to be questioned; this took place at least four or five times, as I recall—it was a brutal process and I grew more upset with every round of questioning.

I hadn't been in charge of what had happened with the money; though checks had always been made out to me, I signed them over to my partner. My jaw dropped when the Assistant Attorney asked,

"Wally ... do you realize how badly your business partner screwed you?"

I hadn't and when he went into the gory details, I could

hardly stomach it. In fact, I started crying. At the end of the day, though, I had nobody but myself to blame for my situation at the time. Despite his dedication to seeming like a decent person, the process dragged out unnecessarily because my partner wouldn't plead guilty.

What began in 2008 lasted until my sentencing in 2013. I'd aged significantly in those five years—as a fugitive of my own mind. I was hardly sleeping, my weight was out of control and my marriage was crumbling, brick by brick, with every day that inched closer to me going to prison.

I was an addict with no money, a failing marriage and dwindling friendships. My sentencing finally made the newspaper ... to my benefit, the government had reduced their sentencing request to 30 months. My partner got a six-year sentence. The government wanted to give him 11 years but was forced to make his lower to match our sentences.

When I testified against him, he acted entirely baffled; he truly believed he'd done nothing wrong. He'd self-deceived to the point where he actually *believed* himself. I realized at that moment—that could have so easily been me.

As part of my sentencing hearing, the judge read aloud some of the statements of character I'd received. I'd petitioned the last few people on earth who had a semblance of belief in me to write a letter; they were generous ... even when I could hardly get on my own team.

As part of the process of pleading guilty to a crime, a

defendant must give an allocution—a statement accepting responsibility for what they did that expresses remorse for the pain and damage they caused. That was the first time in my 45 years on the planet that I blamed nobody but myself for what had happened and accepted full responsibility for my behavior. It took me a while to get through it because I was sobbing as I tried to get every word out of my mouth as intelligibly as possible.

Even my lawyer ended up bonding with me throughout the process—we'd been through five years of hell together, after all. He took up for me with the judge, saying, "Sending him to prison for even a short time wouldn't be necessary, as he wasn't trying to steal money from banks and had been a 'good citizen' up to that point in life. I can attest—he's learned his lesson."

The kindness of these people throughout the process helped me take radical responsibility—for my actions, for being dishonest and for hurting good people. In the end, the judge handed out a 14-month sentence to me, which was what my attorney felt I would end up with once we started working with the government. They wanted me to at least serve some time in prison ... to make an example of me and to deter others from doing what I did.

By the end of it all, I'd made it out—by the skin of my teeth—yet again.

***

On the day I left for prison, my best friends, Paul and

David, *chauffeured* me to Forrest City, Arkansas. It was the most somber, comedic, two-day trip of my entire life. We drove to FCI Forrest City around Labor Day weekend. We packed snacks, stayed in a hotel, laughed, and bonded through long silences. With every mile we traveled away from the DFW area, I left the turbulence of the past few years behind ... wondering if prison would be enough to get my attention and catalyze real change—fearing it wouldn't.

We had no idea what to expect when we arrived at the lifeless gray and brown brick penitentiary complex that would house the next year of my life. As soon as we pulled up, we stopped the car and stepped out. Just as we closed the doors, we heard a loud, commanding voice yell, "Freeze! Don't move! Get back into your cars!"

With wide eyes, we looked at each other—confused. In our peripheral vision, we caught a glimpse of two guards with shotguns walking two prisoners in shackles down the front sidewalk.

We waited as the prisoners were ushered into the front of the building, then stepped out of the car again and walked into the prison entrance for our final goodbyes. I figured it would be the last time I saw anyone for several months. Stacie was in no place to visit me—or to bring the kids—and all the women I'd been seeing on the side rightfully hated me. I hugged my buddies for a long time and surrendered to the weight of the reality I'd created with my own terrible choices.

Then processing began—day one of 366 days in prison. While I was resolute on the outside—on the inside, I felt like the biggest loser of all.

Prison was scary as hell for a first-timer like me—and I was only at the Forrest City prison camp. While there was no fence and we could come and go as we pleased within the complex, we had to be there for headcount ... and there was no adjusting to the culture.

While on the outside, everyone is innocent until proven guilty, in prison, everyone is guilty until proven innocent. If you're there, you're a criminal and you'll be treated as such, stripped of your belongings, your dignity, your identity and your rights. And for what it's worth, that's how it should be. It's a prison, not a vacation club.

One of the biggest adjustments of all was having inadequate healthcare options. There were too many bodies to care for; if any of us got sick, there was a waiting list. When we finally got in to see a physician, we were never taken seriously; at least five men died during my year-long stay.

Equally as bad were those with crippling mental health issues that were made worse by long periods of isolation. Most of us didn't have family come for a visit, though I was fortunate to have friends come and see me. Throughout my entire stay, Stacie never brought the kids to see me. I didn't understand at the time, but I realized many years later how much I had hurt her and that hurt put her in a position of not wanting to help me in any way if she didn't have to. Desperate for connection, a person in prison can only build relationships with those similar enough to them. I found a few other Christians while I was there.

When I first arrived, I didn't have any shoes. One of the kindest things the group did for me was to provide me with shower shoes, bath supplies and a pair of used size 15 sneakers that ended up being a huge hookup for me during my first month there. That's the way we tithed in prison— we'd buy new things to help new inmates get set up in "skid row," a set of bunk beds that sat at the front of the prison barracks where all the noise, lights and action were for 24 hours a day. That's where all new inmates go when they first arrive at the prison camp until they can be put into an open bed in one of the cells.

In the beginning, no one can sleep. They are put in a six-by-eight cinder block cell with a bunk bed. The mattresses are four inches thick with no pillows, two sheets and only one blanket. Each person gets one locker where they can store what they acquire from the commissary and through the work program. The best a person can hope for is a good *celly*.

I, unfortunately, had a terrible initial cellmate. He was a pimp and heroin dealer from St. Louis who was known for storing contraband. At one point, he snitched on me for something I didn't do. As a result, I got sent to the fishbowl, a room with six beds that puts an inmate in even bigger jeopardy of getting into trouble because there are more things people can do that might get a person sent to the SHU (Special Housing Unit) for isolation as punishment.

In prison, even if a person is not responsible for an infraction, if it happens in their space, they are held accountable until they prove themselves innocent. Shortly after, my cellmate, who was responsible for bringing cigarettes, tobacco, phones and alcohol into the prison, was woken up in the night and strip-searched.

Naturally, everyone thought I'd snitched on him—even though I hadn't. When he got caught one week later— thankfully after I'd left the fishbowl—he was placed in the SHU. Had the incident happened one week earlier, I would have been put in solitary until they found out I wasn't guilty and as they are usually in no rush to help inmates clear their name, it would have most likely been a long stay.

This is not uncommon with trips to the SHU; most guys come back much thinner and more stressed out than before they were sent in. Suffice it to say that as bad as prison is, it's nothing compared to the loneliness and isolation of being in solitary confinement.

Fortunately, God was looking out for me and I was put in a new cell with a great guy named Ernie. He showed me how to get through the inevitable loneliness of birthdays and holidays until he was released.

To keep my head on straight, I started working out more.

Surprisingly, they had decent workout equipment, with a couple of treadmills and fitness classes. We had basketball courts and areas where groups played handball and pickleball. Raising my heart rate correlated directly with improving my mood, which progressively worsened until I was launched into deep grief, where God finally got my attention.

Up until that point, I'd had a pretty horrible relationship with my higher power. Catholic shame ran deep and had since my consecration as a little kid. I'd never really understood most of the traditions of the Church. When I was sitting in church with my father, in front of the entire congregation, I was told to accept Christ by drinking his blood.

"Drink his blood?!" I responded. "Yuck!" I said ... trying to earn a hearty laugh. Some people did laugh, but a sovereign silence fell over everything when my father disproportionately reacted by giving me a stern, fear-inducing look.

To escape his scary, silent rage, I crawled under the pew to hide. But there was no hiding from my dad's anger. It followed me wherever I went, which certainly impacted my faith ... all the way up to adulthood, when I was sitting in my prison cell, wondering about the mercy of God. I knew there was no way out of my scenario without consequences. While God might redeem me, no one else was inclined to let me off the hook and truthfully, I can't say I blamed them.

This was made clear on February 14th, 2014, when I received a notification of divorce from Stacie via email. I had signed the divorce paperwork before I left for prison, knowing that when I finally got out, life would be entirely different. Later that year, I left Forest City with 54 cents to my name and nothing more than the clothes on my back—a white T-shirt, a pair of gray shorts with a belt made of one sneaker shoestring and one boot string and the socks and sneakers on my feet. I had no money and no guarantee for a great future outside the grace others were willing to extend to me.

On the day I left, I walked out into the bright sun to see the same vehicle that had dropped me off. Paul and David were there to greet me and take me to my married friends' house—Jay and Amber Kinder. They let me sleep in their guest room, eat their food, live in their home and drive their car. If it were not for them, I'm not sure how I would have survived.

The first night I stepped over the threshold of their home, it felt like the nightmare was over. For the first time in years, I could relax. I enjoyed the longest shower I've ever taken, indulged in the most delicious supper I've ever tasted and slept soundly through the night—feeling more gratitude for my present than fear for my future.

I figured I was at a pivotal moment where I had to trust God. I had nothing else to lean on. And as I did, I found adequate support for each day. After a few days, I was given my job back by Jay and his partner Michael Reese and entrusted with much more than I deserved. It's important to note that Jay and Mike loaned money to me while I was in prison to help me take care of my family. Because of Jay and Mike's generosity, Stacie and the kids were able to stay in our home and live there without interruption.

Once I was on my feet financially, I transitioned out of Jay and Amber's house into my colleague Scott Cameron's rental house. He was a fellow real estate agent and former neighbor who helped me with places to live until I could find a long-term living situation. As well, he and his wife, Shera, lent me money to buy a car for myself. It's safe to say that I was one of the luckiest felons in the world and that God was surely looking out for me.

This is not to say the mental struggle was always easy. Though I had a bright, newfound faith in my life, my brain was having trouble adapting to life outside prison. My complex trauma from childhood was relentless and would rear its ugly head through the symptoms of panic and dread attacks. And even though I was home, I wasn't entirely free to live my life or make choices.

To ensure I maintained good behavior, I was put on three years' probation—which meant I had to check in with my probation officer frequently, specifically, any time I had to travel for work. If I left the state, I was required to fill out paperwork and get approval. Additionally, even though my offense was not drug-related, I was required to get a *piss test* every month for the first year to make sure I wasn't doing drugs. This was especially *fun* because I had to do it with my probation officer standing right next to me, waiting to obtain my urine sample.

Though I was trying to move forward, I could not escape my past; according to the government, I was still a criminal and plainly speaking, a significant part of me still felt like one.

While I'd been humbled through prison and hoped I would do better moving forward, not even I was convinced that the punishment would be enough to keep me from returning to my bad behaviors in the long run.

Though I didn't have words for it at the time, I knew, on an intuitive level, the addictions I had could not be broken by external consequences because they were rooted in a deeper issue. The prison system is a temporary fix to long-term criminal activity because it compounds the internal shame and fear that drive addictive and illegal behaviors. This meant that even though I had a second chance to rebuild my life from the ground up, I didn't have the skill set. Despite my efforts to focus on my strengths at work, my mental highs and lows kept me distracted from everything and made it complicated to build the one thing I needed most—strong, sustained relationships in every area of my life.

Rebuilding trust with my children felt almost impossible

at first. I was confident Stacie didn't have the best things to say about me when I wasn't around, based on the way my kids would sheepishly look at me any time we were together. Even worse was the fact that I'd become a stranger to them while we were separated. To them, I was just their noxious criminal father who had yelled at them for several years before being absorbed into the prison system. I'd become even worse than my father, which was a hard pill to swallow.

It sent me into deep reflection about whether I would ever be loved for real in this

lifetime and I began to desperately crave the intimacy of partnership while recognizing I

probably wasn't ready. I determined I would just leave it with God and it would happen when

the time was right—it would happen.

And then I met Meredith.

Something Lost, Something Gained

My love affair with Meredith began at a business seminar I was speaking at in Dallas, TX. It wasn't necessarily the beginning of a popcorn and Twizzlers rom-com, but there was something sweet about it. I was still adjusting to *living* in the world again, so I was on my *best* behavior–and I certainly looked the part! I'd scrounged together what little money I had to look presentable, hoping a professional opportunity would present itself; a romantic opportunity was the furthest thing from my mind. So, when Meredith and I casually exchanged greetings, I thought little of it, primarily because Meredith was married and I was committed to no longer having affairs with married women. That was until three weeks later ...when she spontaneously connected with me on Facebook.

What began as occasional friendly phone calls and *catching up* led to longer discussions full of intimate details about our lives. I expressed the tumult of being recently divorced and she confided in me about her failing marriage, noting that she would soon be separated, and then divorced, from her husband. Having made my first real connection in a long time, I had no inclination to play by *the rules* if Meredith was *truly* getting a divorce. It took several months of prodding and questioning, but eventually she told me the process was finalized and that we could move forward with our relationship.

I justified what many would call *poor* or *forced* timing by saying our love came *just in the nick of time.* Additionally, we were older, so I rationalized that I didn't have room to be picky. I'd never felt such a spark with anyone—especially not in my first marriage, no fault of Stacie; Meredith made me feel like I was on cloud nine.

The closer we got, the higher the highs became. I wanted to be in love so badly that I overlooked any sign of trouble. *So what* if she'd get mad if I forgot to call or called later than

I said I would—I could live with her criticisms. *So what* if she was passive-aggressive—we all have things we need to work on. I took it as a compliment that she kept a close eye on my Facebook and was on the defensive side when it came to my being friends with other women.

After all, Meredith knew *all of me*. She knew that I'd spent years cheating on my wife. I was *sure* she meant well and *that's* why she'd call or try to message every female I was in communication with ... to *make sure* I wasn't lying. I was in such an unhealthy place I couldn't distinguish these behaviors as red flags until our fighting became more frequent and aggressive and slowly started to spin out of control.

After our relationship devolved into incessant screaming matches, I began to say things like, "If this doesn't change, I'm leaving." "If the fighting doesn't stop—I'm out of this." "I can't deal with this for another second. This has to be the last time."

And it would get better for a while—especially after every one of my threats to leave was met with euphoria and a panic-inducing announcement that Meredith *was pregnant*. The first time she told me we were *expecting*, my anger and resentment immediately melted and making up felt exhilarating.

After the third *false positive*, I began to wonder if Meredith was lying to me. I considered sitting her down and giving her a safe space, to tell the truth. If she had been lying, I wanted to wipe the slate clean—after all, I understood lying; I'd been doing it my whole life.

At the same time, I was pretty dedicated to hiding from the truth—I just didn't want to know, so with complicity, I decided to remain distracted.

To keep our minds busy, Meredith and I planned a vacation together to her parents' house in Florida. I met her mom, dad and sister. On that trip, she confirmed with her family that she'd left her husband and that I was the new guy in town. That week, we re-facilitated the idea that everything was *more than fine* between us. And we sealed the trip after returning home by getting tattoos together that read, *You are the love of my soul* in Arabic.

I had little reason to believe Meredith was cheating on her husband with me and I never imagined she was cheating on both of us with a third guy. In retrospect, something that seemed like a win was actually one of the biggest losses of my life. It ended up siphoning my money, energy and time. And yet it was almost impossible to leave her.

Meredith was beautiful.

Meredith was crazy.

Meredith was a control freak.

And ... I was completely consumed by her.

Imagine my devastation when I learned that everything she'd told me, other than the names of the people in her family and where she lived, was a complete and utter lie.

For almost five straight years, the woman who I'd asked to marry me (who'd accepted my proposal and a diamond engagement ring) had deceived me at every turn.

It was more than I could bear.

In the fall of 2019, I found out that Meredith had never divorced her husband. I was in Austin, Texas, at the time with some friends of mine from college to watch my good friend Herb Hand coach in the Texas vs. LSU Game of the Week on ESPN.

I learned this bit of information from Meredith's sister, who told me she was surprised I hadn't noticed Meredith's toxic and unfaithful patterns sooner, noting she was just *that way*. That's when I realized ... I really didn't know the extent of it. All I knew was that when it came to liars, I had met my match—and the truth was unbearable.

This shocking revelation sent Meredith and me spiraling into a series of fights that were so traumatic I could hardly function. Within one month, she sent me more than 430 emails. As a result, I blocked her on everything and changed my number twice. Both times, she found the new number within one hour. Any time I'd answer the phone, it'd be a barrage of verbally abusive language. But she didn't stop there. Eventually, she went scorched earth and started reaching out to my family, friends, clients and business associates. She was determined to ruin my reputation, so I figured the smartest thing I could do was hire an attorney to address her defamation of my character.

Our battle devolved into a court case so gruesome and dishonest it was unbelievable. Throughout more than 50 pages of false accounts, she said that I'd been aggressive during sex and that I had been physically threatening to her and her family on more than one occasion.

As a result, we got an order to stay away from each other. Because I wanted her to leave me alone as long as possible, I had the attorney subpoena her husband to come to court— and that made her go silent *for a while*. Over the course of a year, I spent more than $8,000 in attorneys' fees and travel trying to stave her off. I also lost what little sanity I'd managed to salvage after prison.

While cutting my losses was devastating, I knew I had to free myself from the last four-plus years of my life—a toxic whirlwind of manic highs, dismal lows and countless deceptions from the woman I wanted to spend the rest of my life with. I rationalized that some part of me should have felt empowered in walking away, but the reality was that my mental health was at an all-time low. I coped through the unmanageable days in throbbing emotional pain ... until I couldn't tolerate the soreness any longer. I was desperate for relief and it was this distress that led me to my darkest hour.

On a cool October night in 2019, I felt so exhausted, withered and fragile that I'd lost my will to live. As much pain, sadness, guilt and shame as I'd experienced over the previous 50 years, I finally got to a place where I couldn't withstand one more second of it. Though everything around me felt hazy, one thing was clear ... I wanted to die.

I was ready to die.

So I sat in the front room of my dark apartment, running my fingers over the smooth leather of my favorite chair, thinking,

I could overdose.

I could steal one of my friend's guns.

I could hang myself.

I could threaten the police.

I could drive off a bridge.

I could—

Until suddenly ... an image of Little Wally crossed my mind.

I'd lived my entire life being afraid of my father, but if I'd lost him as a child, there's no way I would have understood that. I was so influenced by shame that I would have blamed myself. Having become a greater disappointment than my father to my own children, they were the only reason I could think to stay alive.

Even if they hated me and wanted nothing to do with me, their faces crossed my mind and their innocence—and that of my inner child—helped me pick up the phone and make a call. *I needed help. I needed out.* I needed to cut my losses. I was below rock bottom; this was the bottom of the bottom.

I could either take radical responsibility and make a good

life or continue down a path that would only lead to death. As the phone rang, I waited for my aunt and uncle on the other end to pick up. When they finally answered, all the blood rushed back into my cheeks and my heart started pounding. I was alive. I was still alive.

And when they asked me to come out to New Hampshire to help them while my uncle recovered from knee replacement surgery, I began to consider that in the midst of tremendous loss—I could *choose* my gains.

My first gain was the fact that I *had* my family, even if they couldn't fully forgive me at the time. Additionally, I was doing well in my career and my professional relationships were healthier than ever. Moreover, I had my faith and the newfound gratitude that *I, Wally Bressler, was alive*. Which meant I still had time left—to pull myself up by the bootstraps and thrive beyond my circumstances. For the first time throughout my series of losses, fallouts and failures, I was walking into the next chapter of my life with an enduring desire—*to heal*.

6

REBUILDING FROM ROCK BOTTOM

Finding Refuge

I n the winter of 2020, I made the bravest decision of my life. I decided to go to counseling and take my mental health seriously. I found a provider who was a specialist in dialectical behavior therapy—a form of cognitive-behavioral therapy that focuses on talk therapy and mindfulness methods. I paid to be extensively tested for chemical imbalances and for all the appropriate introductory tests I would need for proper intake with my therapist.

Through the tests, I found out that I was an introvert, which was shocking to me, as I was confident my love for the spotlight was a reflection of my authentic desires. But some later digging revealed this was a front I put up to *protect* myself from rejection, abandonment and fallout. Once I learned to settle into myself more, I began to recognize that I was *very, very sad and extremely angry.*

In the beginning, these realizations were enough to sustain my interest in the treatment program, but over time, I realized the person I was working with was not a good fit. I needed someone assertive who was going to hold me accountable, someone who wouldn't lead with "What do you want to talk about today?"

So my search began for an excellent mental health practitioner. Anyone who has ever been in therapy knows the transition can be difficult. No one particularly likes telling their story over and over again or having to familiarize themselves with several people before finding a suitable option. However, to find the necessary sense of refuge it takes to heal—every person must. To my disadvantage, a few months passed and the coronavirus pandemic was overwhelming the nation.

The one thing I really liked about therapy—that kept me accountable—was meeting in person. But for the health benefit of everyone, behavioral health professionals were transitioning to meeting portals like telehealth. Because the pandemic was so turbulent for everyone, most providers had month-long waiting lists for an intake session. Though it was frustrating, I was dedicated to finding what I needed. This was a major test of my patience. Those who know me know that *Wally Bressler doesn't wait in line for anything.* I've always been restless, the first to show up, the most determined to stay and the last to leave. I'm hard-headed.

But I took hope in those qualities. The fact that they'd

been powerful enough to lead to my downfall gave me hope that they would lend to my rebuilding.

I focused on the things I could control and used the few tools I had in my emotional regulation toolbox to keep me strong until July.

When finally—I found Kelly, *my refuge and strength*.

Kelly had run addiction centers for years; she specialized in family therapy and thrived with *adult children* of addicts and abuse. From the moment we met, we easily connected. We met frequently at first—which I needed; like a buoy in the storm, my sessions with Kelly not only saved me from the relentless deep, but they also saved my life. Though I *wanted to want* to live, though I was *desperate always to be desperate* to get better, the specter of suicidal thoughts still stole my sleep and made me afraid of myself. Kelly picked up on this and instead of beginning every meeting with, *what do you want to talk about?* She would ask me, *Wally, do you feel safe?*

The truth was ... I didn't know. Establishing a sense of safety with myself felt inconsistent. Sometimes, I was rock solid; I was confident I could depend on myself. Other times, I felt unstable, with a constantly shifting mood, like anything could come along and bowl me over. In those moments of feeling unsafe, Kelly would make me promise not to hurt myself.

She'd give me specific homework to focus on that would keep my mind from ruminating on the painful, dark cycles that haunted me. It was the most arduous time in my

50-plus years of living because the chaos that had always manifested externally was now contained. I was forced to go inward, to the source of my pain and *feel* everything I had put off feeling since childhood— the neglect, the abuse, the molestation, the repercussions of my lying, my addictions, the downfall of my marriage, the death of my parents, the loss of my business, being put in federal prison and the sheer hell Meredith had brought into my life. It was all demanding to be considered, processed and sorted.

The demand this placed on me mentally, emotionally and psychologically was both necessary and more than my body could wring out all at once.

The plan my dietician gave me was the only thing keeping me stabilized. I needed a routine in place to be able to function. The memories that surfaced were horrible and haunting and keeping my life together externally compounded the severity of everything. There was no room to break down between sales calls and if I allowed myself to cry between meetings, I knew I wouldn't stop. I would sleep between Zoom calls just to numb the enduring pain that overwhelmed my physiological state. It ached in my temples, was caught in my throat and was heavy in my chest.

I had what Kelly referred to as *therapy hangovers*. Tuesdays were my time to unpack my baggage in the afternoon and then I'd go to bed and sometimes sleep until the next day. This was due in part to Kelly's gentle assertiveness in helping me heal but also to her pointing me toward personal accountability. I had to face every lie I'd told, every innocent person I'd hurt and accept that some of these were things I could only learn from.

While I believe in a redeeming God who works everything out for our good, I've learned humans are not that gracious; some things cannot be tangibly redeemed in this lifetime and I had to become OK with that. Kelly taught me how to have compassion for myself about the things I could not redeem, especially relationships with the women I'd hurt in the past. She helped me identify patterns in my romantic relationships that stemmed from a tumultuous childhood, namely the issue of people-pleasing. This led to Kelly suggesting several resources for me, from *Codependent No More* by Melanie Beattie, to *Attached: The New Science of Attachment and How It Can Help You Find—and Keep—Love* by Amir Lavine and Rachel Heller.

Together, Kelly and I started unpacking my past relationships through the lens of attachment theory. Through multiple resources, I learned that attachment theory differs from codependency theory in that it breaks down relating into two categories, *secure* and *insecure*. Within the *secure* category are those with a *secure* attachment style. These are usually people who were raised in stable homes and got their needs met with little struggle throughout childhood.

Because attachment style begins forming as early

as infancy, it's safe to assume a *secure* person had a lot of bonding time with both their parents from the time of birth and throughout their most integral developmental years. Those with *insecure* attachment styles were not as fortunate. Their dysfunctional way of relating can be broken down into two categories, *anxious* and *avoidant*.

The anxiously attached person usually had difficulty feeling settled as a child due to ongoing neglect, abuse, or abandonment. As a result, they grew up believing survival equates to *not* being left. In turn, they often pander to people who are not good partners. They tolerate bad behavior, or arguably worse—they commit their lives to people they don't love because they are desperate for security.

Out of the two insecure attachment styles, the *anxiously attached* are the most aligned with the traditional definition of a *codependent* (someone preoccupied with the acceptance and validation of others to an addictive measure).

Desperate to maintain relationships, *anxiously attached* individuals over-give, over-love and smother without meaning to—which too often leads to the thing they fear the most, namely abandonment. If paired with a *securely* attached person, there's occasionally room for grace when the anxious partner's desperation for reassurance surfaces. But this is rarely the case if they are dating an *avoidant* partner who leans away from intimacy and would be deterred by such behavior.

Those with *avoidant* attachment styles typically grew up

in homes where adverse circumstances taught them to only depend on themselves. Unlike the anxiously attached, they stopped waiting on the parent who never came back and lived out the message *I can and I prefer to do it all by myself (because then no one can threaten my autonomy or hurt me)*. Avoidant partners crave emotional distance and can be hesitant about commitment. They are often characterized in movies as the brooding, reserved and somewhat cold lover who refuses to return affection or communicate how they *really* feel.

While Hollywood romanticizes the chase between one partner leaning in while the other pulls away, this very real cycle is actually quite damaging in personal relationships. Popular psychology and social media buzz about this dysfunctional dance between two insecure lovers, coin it *the ancient avoidance trap*.

While in the trap, the anxious person is voraciously hungry for affection—desperate to meet their unfulfilled needs (usually from childhood); and they will pursue the attention of the *avoidant* ... who feels paralyzed by the demand and can only retreat.

Even if the avoidant partner deeply loves the anxious partner, their nervous systems become paralyzed by the excessive need for engagement. So they only share themselves incrementally, which leaves both partners feeling triggered and unfulfilled.

In *Attached*, Lavine and Heller note that "Basically, secure people feel comfortable with intimacy and are usually warm and loving; anxious people crave intimacy, are often preoccupied with their relationships and tend to worry about their partner's ability to love them back; avoidant people equate intimacy with a loss of independence and constantly try to minimize closeness."[24]

And it's important to understand that none of them are *wrong* because all are reasonably trying to get their needs met in their personal relationships.

Reading *Attached* opened me up to the notion that I had an anxious attachment style. This is a no-brainer because I've had trust issues most of my life—anxiety, paranoia and a boisterous personality that has played gatekeeper to letting people in.

When it came to dating, things would be fantastic in the early stages—I'd be funny and seemingly available and I'd attach quickly. Then 60 to 90 days down the road, my hidden identity would remind me that I'm *not good enough, not deserving of these things, not worthy.*

Then I would go numb and leave—completely vanishing on some really great partners with no explanation. Then I'd bury it ... because I hated myself so much; I could never summon the strength to take radical responsibility. I was driven solely by the need for significance, so ... I was on to the next one.

---

24 Levine, Amir, and Rachel Heller. *Attached*, 2011.

Kelly emphasized that the false identities I was living presented two extremes. There was the *nice guy* who claimed to want to help people but was essentially inauthentic because his *kindness* was primarily a survival strategy. Then there was the *master manipulator* who could dial down the empathy when he was pathologically lying to people. And the only thing that could make an impact on either persona was radical self-compassion. We began working on techniques for emotional regulation, which were challenging at first—especially because I had trouble naming precisely what I was feeling. Kelly advised me to take note of when I was overthinking things. *Getting in my head too much* was a tell that I wasn't in my heart, that I needed to *feel my feelings*. I hadn't realized that much of the anxiety I was experiencing was a defense mechanism to keep me from processing the pain of past trauma.

In *The Tao of Fully Feeling*, Pete Walker writes, "Feelings and emotions are energetic states that do not magically dissipate when they are ignored. Much of our unnecessary emotional pain is the distressing pressure that comes from not releasing emotional energy. When we do not attend to our feelings, they accumulate inside us and create a mounting anxiety that we commonly dismiss as stress."[25]

I've done enough research on trauma to know that *crying is the goal*. If we can will ourselves to cry, we can work through

---

25 Walker, Pete. *The Tao of Fully Feeling*, 2015.

the tension of grief. In turn, we become *more* functional overall; our vacillating emotional states stabilize–making them less intimidating to manage.

In the beginning, allowing myself to cry would have wiped me out for a whole day or even the weekend. But I learned that it's actually my wisest preventative strategy. The faster I can get to crying, the less time I spend experiencing surface emotions that uproot nothing and keep me distracted from my daily responsibilities. The more I relax into my emotions and let them pass through me, the better I feel.

After nine long months of hard work, I began to experience full days without pain from time to time. I'd be able to regulate emotionally until really impactful situations would happen and then I'd lose my footing.

It took more than a year to feel strong enough in myself to navigate the really difficult things. But after I had the tools in place and committed to using them regularly ... I realized that I had transformed as a person. The switch had finally flipped. The disconnect between my heart and mind had been bridged and both had equal validity in my life and decision-making. My inner dialogue dramatically shifted, which led me to feel truly hopeful about my future.

By my 53rd birthday, I felt fully redeemed and proud of myself. For more than five decades, I'd never finished anything. Finally, I had worked through many things that were holding me back in the most important areas of my life, which enabled me to make massive strides in my business, personal life and relationships.

This was due in part to establishing strong communication skills that were heart-centered, as opposed to a sales pitch. All my life, I'd been a really good *talker* ... but I never said much of integrity or value because I was hiding who I really was with the art of words.

When Kelly initially implied I wasn't a great communicator, I balked at the thought; had we not had excellent banter? I was being *so transparent*. But midway through our work together, I began to realize that while most of what I was saying was transparent, it wasn't very vulnerable.

This came to my attention when Kelly had said something in one of our sessions that struck a nerve and I reactively disconnected our video session. I'd been feeling emotionally drained and just didn't have the energy or the skill set to say what I needed to say.

Before I owned my behavior, I spent some time spiraling in shame and pouting like a child.

What had I done? Kelly has helped me so much. Did I sabotage the only thing that was making me better?

When I hopped onto the video call for our next session with my tail between my legs, she was professional, kind and clear. Furthermore, she commended me for being honest about my frustration; *at least I hadn't lied! That was progress!*

Not only did Kelly and my healthy exchange flood me with a

sense of relief, but it also taught me about reconciliation and continuing hard conversations. Relationships don't have to end abruptly. When I brought this up at a later appointment, Kelly offered to help me with *feeling statements*; that way, I'd have a structured way to communicate myself that was less impulsive and ultimately left me feeling empowered. This especially helped when we discussed how to address anxieties and irritations in professional situations when I felt like I was losing my nerve.

Not only did I learn about the benefit of *I* statements, but I also became a more active listener. My newfound integrity with myself and my ability to discern my emotions gave me clarity about how to communicate in difficult moments.

When_____happens, I feel_____; then I tell myself_____ and come to believe_____.

After I felt like I could express myself in a constructive way, I was able to tune in to what the other person was *really* saying, as opposed to leaning into the story I was telling myself. At first, it felt strange to implement and then it became fun, until finally ... it was so natural I didn't have to think about doing it intentionally at all. As a result, the people around me started recognizing my ability to resolve conflict. It made me more peaceful to deal with, so my bonds with others got stronger; people *wanted* to be around me *because* of myself (not despite myself), which dissolved the desire to people-please.

The less performative I became, the more secure my

attachment style became. This set me up to build romantic relationships on my terms. The most shocking discovery of all was learning that *most* of my pursuits were ego- or fear-driven.

Once I got my head on straight, dating became something I considered and casually enjoyed, but it wouldn't capsize me if it didn't work out. My identity was coming into full color. I was no longer buried beneath my mistakes and the things that had been done to me. I had a newfound resiliency, strength and triumphant nature about me.

In the more than 150 counseling sessions I had done with Kelly, I came to acknowledge that I was not a villain. While I'd spent the majority of my life antagonizing myself and everyone around me, I still had plenty of life in which to redeem myself. I could still be the hero of my own story.

After all, every hero has obstacles to overcome on their way to being able to contribute to the greater good. And after I faced and fought off most of the demons that threatened my livelihood from the inside out, I was enthusiastic about offering the most valiant parts of myself up to something greater.

From a healthy, authentic place, I came to learn that I wanted to lift others up by pointing them to their own healing. So, in late 2020, I began to consider all the skills I'd acquired since beginning therapy with Kelly. Then I sat down to write a business plan with Jeff Lopez, cofounder of *Phone Sales Secrets* and a digital marketing expert. His direction and guidance, paired with my vision, yielded a sales endeavor so impactful that it would change my life and the lives of my future clients indefinitely.

7

TRAGICALLY HEROIC

You Are Not Stuck As You Are

I t takes a while for the outside world to reflect the inside. On the trajectory of my recovery, I had to remind myself of this every day as I woke up to the consequences of my actions. In the business world, there were people so livid with me after I got out of prison that I had to delete death threats from social media. People promised me that if I ever returned to New Hampshire, I would be killed. While this was terrifying, a good portion of my suicidal ideation was due to financial circumstances. Though I was back in business, I officially owed the IRS more than one million dollars. Furthermore, I destroyed my credit.

Because Meredith knew all this, I could rest assured that everyone else did, too, which inevitably compounded my internal shame.

Most of my conversations with Kelly revolved around

the practical concern: *Could I ever overcome the social stigma of being a convicted felon?*

Kelly assured me that the answer was *yes*—but suggested that I be patient while waiting for a return on my investment. She reminded me of something I have seen in the sales world time and time again: People *love* a redemption arc—especially in the context of a protagonist who has presented as otherwise, namely *tragic*.

For the most part, we're all familiar with the trajectory of an *epic hero* in traditional storytelling: The protagonist begins with somewhat of a divine *calling*. Then they venture out on a whimsical, exciting, sometimes dangerous journey where they hit moderate resistance over and over and over again until they find themselves in a position of existential questioning—that only a guide, spiritual mentor, or guru can help them through.

Once the guide appears, they counsel the hero while spurring them toward their purpose. Throughout the rest of their travels, they are physically, mentally and emotionally put to the test until they are entirely depleted. Then a grand epiphany or revelation leads them to triumph, bringing the story full circle—and beckoning the hero *home*.

The more unsteady, *tragic hero*, however, hits a few more low points. Namely, the fact that his well-intentioned choices usually turn on him, his fair-weather friends betray him, natural disasters are out to destroy him and the vengeful or mischievous gods deliberately seek to teach him hard lessons—time and again (though he rarely learns).

Furthermore, the journey of the tragic hero often ends in death, or at least in an unsatisfying conclusion. The best thing he gets throughout the entire story is a substantial redemption arc—one that sustains the theme that *Life's not about the destination; it's about the journey.*

It is these wily heroes who are my favorite: The vigilante with values conflicting enough to transform an audience's judgment into mercy; the crook who steals from the rich and lavishes the beggar, who challenges the law of the land in pursuit of true virtue; the stubborn child—tied to the magic of youth so much he's willing to risk the abundance of a life fulfilled just to preserve it; the fool who takes to his journey with a fatal optimism that will only be wrung out of him when *fate* has other plans.

These are the heroes I relate to—ones that celebrate nuance and remind us that despite our deepest desires to be good, despite our greatest efforts to present as righteous ... we are all undeniably, tragically *flawed*.

We are also largely out of control of what tragedy might befall us. The hard part of being human is that sometimes— there is no huge reward at the end. We are not guaranteed a life of comic relief. So when the wolves are at our door or darkness falls upon our back, when the food is all gone, the money is siphoned and the rain comes—we can still find *hope* despite our circumstances.

Hope because who we become in the midst of terrible occurrences is what defines our legacy. Hope because no matter how badly we mess it up or how deeply we are harmed or oppressed, we have complete control over *one thing*— and that *one thing* is ourselves, our beliefs, our thoughts, our behaviors and our responses. And sometimes—those things can be rewired to bring us fortune and redeem our circumstances.

In my life, that has been the case. But if there's anything a global pandemic has taught us, it's that ... we are not invincible. We are not immune. We are not guaranteed survival, success, wealth, happiness, or prosperity. That is why it is our responsibility to cultivate a sharp mind, bold hope and a resilient spirit—right now. Today. In the present moment, which is all we have.

Since getting out of federal prison and rebuilding my life from the ground up, I have adopted a new saying: *Even when I don't win, I win.* In keeping with my beliefs about the stories we tell ourselves, I no longer have any interest in considering myself a *failure.* I don't talk to myself that way because even when I experience hard times due to my own mistakes (and I still do), I decide everything is as it should be and I look for every shred of evidence that this is true.

To live a heroic life of virtue, we must embrace the *win* of present transformation and the responsibility of personal refinement. Our character will always be more important than the end result; and it will always help us navigate our outcomes. Therein, the only hopelessness that really exists in the world is self-determined and self-cultivated; to forfeit the opportunity of a great life due to emotional pain or the inability to reconcile with the past is a self-sustaining tragedy. By releasing control over the outcome and taking responsibility for *how we live* ... we take the reins of our own redemption arc.

Spoiler alert: We *all* die in the end, but I believe, outside of external tragedy, we have some degree in determining how we go ... namely, whether we leave this life *fulfilled*. My parents not only died from their vices—they died every day they didn't stand up and fight for their mental health, our family and our future. And unfortunately—their trajectory is the norm.

Too many of us decay inside the death grip of our vices. We overwork, overeat, never rest, never sleep, pass on exercise, don't invest in our communities, don't connect with ourselves and rarely stop to consider how this affects our health. In turn, we forfeit the opportunity to live lives of contribution, wellness and abundance.

Some of us will go peacefully, but some will go tragically. And we hope, by the grace of God, it will be the former; we grieve more deeply when it is the latter. Our reality is that none of us live above human conditions or the suffering of the world that endures, despite our best efforts. And all of these truths do not make us exempt from taking personal responsibility—to turn from our mistakes, to *make something beautiful* with our lives, which are ultimately, undoubtedly *gifts*.

So as I navigate the other side of recovery—where life still happens, triggers still exist and pain is still real—I find my own journey as a tragic hero insanely messy ... and beautiful. I accept that while I strive to live every day *transformed*, that growth is not linear.

As much as I have recovered, I am not proud enough to think I am above my addictions. If there's anything my false sense of security in material things has taught me, it's that we are all only a few steps away from losing it all and life is much more fragile than we think.

This is all the more reason to embrace our rations—and be genuinely grateful for the good that is here to celebrate and the bad that is here to teach us something. Only when we approach our lives this way can we establish a sense of pride in a life lived well and celebrate that *we are never stuck as we are* because we have the power to overcome.

And as the world around us catches up to mirror our internal beliefs (as it so generously does), we can celebrate our tragic heroism as we lean into our personal character arcs—again and again and again.

The Hero's Motivation: Finding Your Why

Whether valiant or entirely illogical—heroes throughout literature are developed with a resounding *why* that inspires their journey. Be it to find the magic beans, fight the angry dragon, storm the castle, save the princess (by climbing her hair), sail the far seas, slay Poseidon, or poison an evil king to overthrow his kingdom—the hero of every story *always* knows their *why*.

Now, sometimes this *why* is wrapped up in a narrative about legacy. It has to do with who their parents were (or were not), their socioeconomic class and what they had (or had not), or protecting the people of their homeland. Other times, this *why* is inspired by romantic love or the hope of finding love—by pursuing a path of wild adventure and unforeseeable circumstances.

Finally, some heroes are motivated by attributes alone—they might want to gain academic knowledge, philosophical insight, physical strength, magical powers, or ancient wisdom. But no matter their inspiration, their journeys only begin and successfully conclude if they have an established *why*.

Now, *epic heroes* are developed to keep their eye on the prize; they (usually) *burn* with purpose. Their fervent passion for their mission is what keeps them on their course when they are looted by mischievous bandits, seduced by mystical sorceresses, or taken captive by evil queens.

The *tragic hero*, however, is the one I find *a lot* more relatable. They are highly distractible, find themselves on alternate missions, are easily tricked and usually find their plans foiled by someone much smarter and more capable than them. Moreover, any awareness of their deficits and efforts to redeem themselves are futile. Tragic heroes often find themselves down and out due to their own foolish mistakes and they can't find their way back because they've forgotten their mission; moreover, they've forgotten *who* they are, *what* they stand for and *how* they live.

Sound familiar? It does to me too. For this motley crew, it takes a heck of a lot more wrong turns to finally *get* going on the right trajectory. Sometimes (if they're lucky), the guidance of a magical guru or mystical healer turns their spirits upright and points them toward their true north again.

It's usually these helping characters that understand the hero enough to be able to recognize what fuels them and therein positions them to point them back toward their *why*.

These are some of my favorite characters because they bring conscience to the hero and instill hope in them when it seems like everything is lost.

This is why I find tragic heroes, like myself especially, need guides, teachers and healers along the way ... namely when it comes to determining and protecting our *why*. It cannot and should not be done alone and it is one of our biggest responsibilities to find safe counsel who we are willing to let speak into those places. I recognize this isn't easy—our *why* is a tender, sacred place, a place where many of us have been bruised. I certainly had been but never realized it until I began my work with Kelly.

When I was a little boy, I wanted so badly to look up to the person who was supposed to be my *hero*. It is the dream of every child to have the quintessential, heroic father who is committed to laying his life down for his kids—no matter the cost.

He wouldn't have had to do big things like fight fires or police injustice or do brain surgery. I just needed him to do the little things like celebrating my birthday with me, coming to my baseball games, teaching me how to be a man and being less punishing toward everyone—especially himself. Unfortunately, that was not my story; that was not my father; that was not the hero I got.

Instead, I watched my father's hatred toward his parents and himself create so much inner turmoil that he became a villain in his own story—the antagonist to his own children. He could have established his *why* early on and determined that he would not contribute to the downfall of his legacy, but he chose instead to surrender the best parts of himself to the worst parts of himself as my siblings and I watched, listened and learned.

While my father circulated jobs to keep the lights on (that

made him miserable and kept us poor for a good portion of my childhood), I always wondered if he'd ever achieve his dream of opening a pizza and sub sandwich shop. I wondered about his *why* and how he'd lost sight of it. I can only imagine that his motivation was never cultivated or encouraged by my grandparents. There was never enough love, resources, or hope in his life to breathe oxygen into the things he desired to accomplish.

As a dismal result, he spent the majority of my upbringing deflating *my* ambitions and dimming the flicker he saw in me—the innate belief that *I could do or be ... anything that I wanted to be.* I was not allowed the luxury of my dreams.

Under my father's roof, one thing remained clear: There was no room for doing things in a non-traditional way. And because I was a boisterous, brazen, clever kid, my potential had no room to expand ... there was only shrinking in my childhood. Standing in the corner with my nose to the wall—*shrinking*, all because a man who did not cultivate his *why* failed to protect, inspire and encourage mine. This was, in my opinion, my father's greatest failure—not protecting the will and dreams of his children; it is all the more reason I will not repeat his mistakes.

***

When coaching clients come to me to break through call reluctance, I challenge them using a series of hard questions, to get to their *why*. And when I do, I learn so much about them, their personal pain, their motivations and their fears.

Some of them have resounding, clear *whys* that don't take a lot of digging, while others can sense *something* driving them physiologically, but they can't identify what it is. "I feel it in my stomach and chest," they'll say. It's usually a warm, fiery sensation like *being lit up*. I work with them to get it as concise and clear as possible until they can put it into a mission statement that will help them determine a sense of direction.

This is especially relieving to clients who have *lost* their sense of direction due to the loudness of external opinions— be it from their parents, families, or society. Part of our work together is drowning out the noise until they can hear their *why* so clearly that it helps guide them forward. It also helps determine which *whys* are not based on strong values, healthy expectations, or *reality*.

I mean, come on. I work in sales ... with all the Jerry Maguires, remember? Of course, I have those clients who start coaching with me without knowing what they're in for. They don't realize that I'm going to dive deep into the fact that most of their motivators are external, material and unsustainable.

As a rule of thumb, a *why* should be sustainable enough to motivate a person through their entire journey. It can't be a short-sighted motivation because buying that sports car that inspires you in your 20s (and most likely sends you into debt) won't still excite you in your 60s—I promise. I like to remind my clients that we live in a consumptive society.

We quickly forget why (and sometimes that) we bought something—almost immediately after we swipe our credit cards.

Furthermore, I've worked with enough people to determine that *external motivators* do not make good *whys* and that to establish great *internal motivators*, we must be in tune with our *whats*.

What motivates you?
What inspires you?
What makes you feel excited?
What makes you feel angry?

When I ask my clients these questions, I get responses such as,

Financial independence motivates me.
Successful entrepreneurs inspire me.
I feel excited when I spend time with my children.
I feel angry when I disappoint a big client.

By using their *whats*, I can then direct them to their *why*.

My why is to be debt-free.
My why is because I was born to be a business owner.
My why is to support my family.
My why is to thrive in client relations.

And this exercise extends beyond business. We can have a central *why* for the many facets of our lives, but to determine our mission and stay the course, we *must* be in tune with them. Additionally, we must surround ourselves with like-minded mentors and peers to remind us why we started on that business venture, weight-loss journey, creative endeavor, or academic pursuit.

Finally, it is imperative that our *whys* are not based on compulsion, shame, or fear. A good indicator of a compulsion-based *why* is when we use (and physiologically feel) the straining word *should*. You may not be truly motivated by things you *should* be motivated by—and this is not only OK, but it's also important to identify.

I should be saving money will never become your sole motivator for saving money. It's disempowering and even if it did encourage you to put away the credit card, the minute you swipe it again, you'd just feel like garbage about yourself.

By now, you've realized that shame begets shame. So when determining your *whats* and *whys*, be honest with yourself and compassionately embrace the motivators that innately inspire you toward success.

A Hero After All

The most tragic part of my heroic journey was never fully being able to embrace the redemptive parts of myself that were fighting to eclipse the consumptive parts. My unmet needs had been left unattended for so long that my life became about devouring everything I could get my hands on instead of fully assessing my innate value and everything I had to offer the world.

Sure, I might have been the kid who was a compulsive liar, an emotional eater and a porn addict, but I was also an empathetic child with a brilliant sense of humor who really *loved* people. There were so many things I deeply valued growing up that were a reflection of my true identity— wholesome things like the way everyone looked in colorful, pointed hats while singing *Happy Birthday* to me, the way the summer night smelled caramelly and sweet at little league baseball games, the way my Snoopy toothbrush fit perfectly into my porcelain toothbrush holder and the way eggs sounded when they were cracked over a frying pan as my father made breakfast.

I have to believe these characteristics of Little Wally are *also* a reflection of who I've always been, even though life, time and pain wrung my innocence right out of me. It is because of this belief that I have been able to define my *why* that fuels the business that I love so much.

For me, *Phone Sales Secrets* is an opportunity to meet people like me, who want to thrive in their dreams as entrepreneurs, but may not have worked through the childhood pain and emotional blocks that are keeping them from their professional potential.

Want to know *what* makes me, Wally Bressler, angry? In

2021 alone, there were more than 27.1 billion dollars of revenue still left on the table that could have influenced the economy if salespeople could have worked through their trauma and insecurities and made a phone call.

I get angry when good people with great intentions remain stunted because they don't have the skill set to work through their baggage. It is this indignation that is deeply interconnected with my desire to *help* people and use my professional skill set to make a difference in the world.

Moreover, I have lived it. I have made *all* the bad choices and mistakes a person can make to upend their lives: from giving way to my vices, to paying the price for bad behaviors, to losing everything then rebuilding from scratch on four separate occasions. I know exactly what it looks like to have patterns of the past impeding my ability to make great decisions for myself and my family. In turn, it has become my *why* to help others peel back the layers so they can pick up the phone and change the trajectory of their lives.

My curriculum is rooted in the concept of *identity*. It challenges my clients to consider that they can still be heroes *after all*—no matter how bleak their businesses look, no matter their starting point, especially when they feel *the most* like a failure and have fallen out of touch with who they really are.

This was the case with my client Brian, who had spent most of his career as a firefighter. Brian was a strong, powerful guy—fearless in so many ways, a true leader and defender of his community, family and friends. By the sight of Brian—with his large, muscular frame and thick, black tribal tattoos—one would have imagined he was not afraid of anything. As someone who has never walked out of a burning building, I found it interesting that Brian was turning to me to give him something he was *missing*. He informed me that he'd transitioned to a part-time career in real estate and was terrified to pick up the phone. Together, we identified that Brian was struggling deeply with call reluctance; as a result, he wasn't getting any prospects.

After 45 days of working with Brian, we were able to identify the fears and insecurities that were being mirrored back to him by his intermittent success in the sales world. As a result, he began cold calling and regular prospecting, which boosted his confidence and grew his business extensively in a short time.

One of the first calls Brian made was to a builder of a $500,000 house. He promised them he'd have the house sold in *no time* with no debilitating anxiety and a newfound confidence that he could get the job done—a complete life and business shift in less than two months!

Similar to Brian was my client, Joel, a digital marketer who wanted to thrive in the social media space. Unfortunately, Joel was afraid of being judged and picked apart by strangers. He hated making videos, live streams and all the requirements it takes to thrive on popular applications.

After six short weeks of working through my curriculum, Joel felt inspired to start his own social media group to share some of the techniques we'd been working through. Almost immediately, it gained a following of 100 people. By the end of our work together, Joel had not only adapted to engaging with commenters in high volumes, but he also worked through his fears of being front and center and now is on a regular posting schedule to effectively grow his business.

Then there was Danielle. Danielle came to me with some truly debilitating hidden identities that were dismantling her business and personal life. A string of untimely deaths and challenging relationships with family members caused her to go into a protective *cocoon* that kept her from accomplishing her dreams. Things had gotten so bad that she wouldn't even take a phone call from her physician to confirm an upcoming appointment until finally, Danielle decided that she'd had enough and chose to take advantage of my courses. By the end of 2021, not only was she prospecting consistently—even throughout a bout of COVID-19—she'd also put together six sales between December 2021 and January 2022. She's currently producing regularly and is positioned to become one of the top agents in her office.

And these are just three examples out of the hundreds of lives that have been changed by the deep, inner work we do through *Phone Sales Secrets*. Every day, I coach clients through the challenging barriers that keep them from seeing their full identity and potential.

I began this work with the dream that I could help others overcome the fear and self-loathing that devastate our present and rob us of our future. My primary goal is to help others understand that if they are willing, intentional, disciplined and brave—they can have successful careers, healthy relationships and a lifetime of happiness, *no matter* how dismal the circumstances.

So again, I'll invite you to say it with me.

I am not a victim.

And neither are you.

It is my hope that we can come together to see ourselves no longer in a negative light due to limiting beliefs, poor judgments and past mistakes, but for the heroes we truly are (no matter how tragic), committed to taking *radical responsibility* for our purpose and unwilling to give up on ourselves and our lives without an ardent, indelible fight.

About Wally

Nominated for *Success Magazine*'s Success 125: One of the 125 Most Influential People in Real Estate that Get Results

Wally Bressler is an ex-con turned life and business coach whose primary goal is to help people realize that they don't have to hit rock bottom to experience radical transformation. In 2021, he began *Phone Sales Secrets*: a company that helps entrepreneurs and salespeople overcome *sales call reluctance*, self-sabotage, and avoidance behaviors. His curriculum consists of personal development techniques that have supported his recovery journey and positioned thousands of clients for success. Bressler has conducted more than 35,000 virtual and live coaching sessions with some of the top real estate professionals in North America. Bressler currently lives in McKinney, TX, where he co-parents his four exceptional children. He is a regular member and volunteer at Crosspoint Church and a dedicated supporter of his community.

CPSIA information can be obtained
at www.ICGtesting.com
Printed in the USA
LVHW081404030922
727555LV00018B/749/J